"Linda DeFruscio has written a comprehensive and enlightening must-read primer for anyone who is beginning their transition from male to female or female to male. Courageous transgender women share obstacles they face as they embark on their journeys to find new places in the world while rediscovering themselves. As they share personal heartfelt stories, a thread of commonality shows the reader the importance of living your truth, loving yourself, and teaching others the importance of tolerance and acceptance. Linda brilliantly peppers these incredible stories by sharing her perspective as their electrologist while also educating her readers on what it means to be transgender."

—**Jeanette Renee**
TLC's *I Am Jazz*

"Linda DeFruscio is a true gift to this world: a successful and talented skin-care professional, exceptional researcher and writer, motivational speaker, outstanding conversationalist, and overall compassionate and considerate woman. In her inspirational work*
Transgender Profiles: Time for a Change, we discover the stories of twenty amazing individuals, their courageous acts of transition, and unforgettable words of advice. Throughout the text, Linda provides us with incredibly valuable medical information, stemming from her impressive breadth of professional experience and personal encounters. Not only does this work open one's eyes and mind to the transgender community, it goes beyond that to remind us of the importance of loving and caring for one another. Thanks to people like Linda DeFruscio, our world is becoming a more accepting and safer place."

—**Andrew J. Safioleas, PharmD, MBA, PRS, RPh**
Inpatient Pharmacist and Music Instructor

"Linda DeFruscio and her colleagues have been helping trans people for quite a while—and there are more of us on the way. This clear, helpful collection tells many of our stories in the irreplaceable and accessible form of brief oral histories; it's also got information about the medical and skin-related services that we may need, that some of us don't understand, and that she both understands and provides. A lot of people will learn a lot from this book."

—**Stephanie Burt**
Professor of English, Harvard University

"*Transgender Profiles* is an in-depth reveal of the transgender world. Linda DeFruscio pulls back the curtain and allows us to witness the difficult decision-making process that patients from all walks of life have chosen to go through. The book makes it clear that, from a very early age, these patients were struggling with the concept of their gender identity. This gender dysphoria is hardwired and has a biologic origin. This is not a choice but must be done at any cost.

As a physician in this field, [I can attest that] the book is a very accurate description of the struggles, failures, and successes within the transgender community. This book will help the reader better understand the transgender community and hopefully lead to a greater degree of tolerance and acceptance."

—**Joseph A. Russo, MD**

"Linda DeFruscio has drawn on her decades of experience providing the most intimate and protracted clinical procedures to paint a vivid and unique portrait of the transgender experience."

—**C.R.Lindley, MD**

Transgender Profiles

Transgender Profiles

Time for a Change

Linda DeFruscio-Robinson

BROWN BOOKS
PUBLISHING GROUP

Transgender Profiles
Time for a Change

Brown Books Publishing Group
16250 Knoll Trail Drive, Suite 205
Dallas, Texas 75248
www.BrownBooks.com
(972) 381-0009

A New Era in Publishing®

Publisher's Cataloging-In-Publication Data

Names: DeFruscio-Robinson, Linda.
Title: Transgender profiles : time for a change / Linda DeFruscio-Robinson.
Description: Dallas, Texas : Brown Books Publishing Group, [2018]
Identifiers: ISBN 9781612549866
Subjects: LCSH: Transgender people—Biography. | Transgender people—Psychology. | Gender nonconformity—Psychological aspects. | Life change events—Psychological aspects. | LCGFT: Biography.
Classification: LCC HQ77.7 .D44 2018 | DDC 306.768092/2--dc23

ISBN 978-1-61254-986-6
LCCN 2017954537

Printed in the United States
10 9 8 7 6 5 4 3 2 1

For more information or to contact the author,
please go to www.LindaDeFruscio.com.

*For Greg, and for transgender people
and communities everywhere.*

"Open your eyes. Look around. There are people in your family or in your circle of friends who are transgender."

—FORMER NAVY SEAL KRISTIN BECK

"In my life I've crossed paths with many different people, and I've seen firsthand what it means to be discriminated against. I've come to realize equality means a lot to people who don't have it and that, as a straight person, I have a responsibility to stand up for gay and transgender people each and every day. We all have to get involved; we all have to give a damn."

—ENTERTAINER AND COFOUNDER OF
TRUE COLORS FUND
(WHICH LAUNCHED THE GIVE A DAMN CAMPAIGN)
CYNDI LAUPER

"Be who you are and say what you feel, because those who mind don't matter and those who matter don't mind."

—DR. SEUSS

"Treat people as if they were what they ought to be, and you help them to become what they are capable of being."

—JOHANN WOLFGANG VON GOETHE

Contents

Stories of Transition

A Note from the Author

This book contains a number of personal anecdotes, both patient cases used with permission and stories others have given me to be included. However, every individual's transgender journey is personal and unique. Several of the individuals described in this book have taken different paths. The decision that was right for them may not be right for someone else, and the hair removal treatments or surgical procedures given here as examples are not meant to be representative.

Transgender individuals considering hair removal or SRS should consult with the appropriate counselors and physicians before committing to any action. Due consideration must be given to the skills of any medical practitioner, as well as the patient's hormones, medications, genetics, age, and any number of other lifestyle factors. Individuals considering SRS should also check the laws of the state and/or country in which they reside in order to ensure compliance.

Any surgical procedure has its risks. In most cases, the corrective procedures that I have seen patients undergo have had successful and fulfilling outcomes, but results vary as to what that means for each patient, and unfortunately, perfection and satisfaction may not be guaranteed.

To anyone engaged in the journey to live with authenticity, I offer my congratulations and my support. Whatever that means for you, may you find peace and joy. You are not alone.

Foreword

Marci L. Bowers, MD

A cultural phenomenon arose in the 1990s that stated simply *Men Are from Mars, Women Are from Venus*. John Gray's "practical guide for improving communication and getting what you want in your relationships" highlighted gender-based differences, suggesting that men and women are fundamentally different and that their respective behaviors are a reflection of those innate differences. Many have argued that the book's purported intention had just the opposite effect, offering seemingly dysfunctional gender-specific replies to everyday relationship conflicts that might be best understood if we existed on the same planet and spoke to one another as equals.

In fact, males and females of the human species share 99.7 percent of the same DNA. Healthy adult men produce estrogen and cis women testosterone. Men indeed have breasts/nipples. Genitals arise from the same original fetal tissues, whether male or female. And women have small clitorises that act like small penises. Especially in the formation of genitalia, there are more than a dozen biological conditions, called intersex, in which the genitals do not form exclusively male or female at birth. The rise of the transgender movement offers hope that we indeed may actually be more alike than dissimilar—biologically. Linda DeFruscio's book helps us to understand the anguish and the reality that is posed by a person facing a transgender struggle—and how so often that struggle includes a prolonged battle to conform, trying, as we all do, to live by what society has told us since our gender assignment at birth, the sole criterion for that assignment being what our respective genitals looked like on day one. As a result, we are all under subtle pressure to live by society's rules and conscriptions for what is masculine and feminine. Often it works, but often it is painful—to us and to those around us—and, ultimately, dysfunctional to live artificially. Moreover, a spectrum of maleness and femaleness makes more sense in nature than a choice of two polar extremes—and gender identity, too, may be represented by diversity along a spectrum from female to male. Living authentic lives leads to greater happiness, and this is the essential goodness that shines through.

Linda's clients' stories are real. The self-discovery is real. The money spent on electrolysis is real (and fascinating!). Funny how fifty or one hundred dollars per session adds up to real money, such that full treatment for hair removal can cost in the tens of thousands of dollars, with hundreds and hundreds of hours spent in the electrologist's chair. It is in these countless hours with clients that stories unfold, recollected and told by Linda. The electrologist becomes a trans girl's best friend, confidante, therapist, and life coach. The day-to-day decisions women go through are considered. The conflict of past weeks or of ongoing relationships is considered. Never is there a dull moment in transition, to the point that once electrolysis, hormones, and surgery are over, there is almost a letdown—a sadness in knowing that such a long climb toward authenticity is finally over.

There is challenge in reading a nontrans person's attempt to generalize or interpret a trans experience. There is still a tendency to succumb to societal gender norms and our own biases. Thus, males motivated to live as females are questioned for hidden sexual underpinnings. Are they still getting erections? When an MTF person stares at another woman, is it sexual? The fact that this question is asked shows that nontrans folk don't get it. Trans women run very low testosterone levels—they are women, and they have female libidos. Yet we rarely question masculine-identified women as to whether they are having sexual thoughts when they stare at another woman.

The perspective that is gained by being transgender and living two lives is most instructive and most hopeful. In a world burdened by gender differences, it is the crossover effect, the experiential learning that comes from birth in one gender and life in the other, that is most instructive and fascinating—and it is worth knowing this extraordinary group of humanity. Linda's accounts give voice to those perspectives and that narrative.

Preface

I'm an electrologist, which is to say I remove unwanted hair from people's faces and bodies. I got into the business when I was very young because my mom was an electrologist. Her office was in our home, and I had the chance to see her at work regularly. I went into a dental studies program after high school and got certified to work as an assistant, but in the end I followed in my mother's footsteps and went to school for electrology, and cosmetology too.

One of my mother's clients was a man by the name of Bart. Bart, who was our neighbor, was a cross-dresser. He was over at our house often, both for his electrolysis sessions and just to visit. He took a liking to me, and when I expressed an interest in starting my own electrolysis business and working from an office in town, he suggested I come with him to a meeting at the Tiffany Club, a social and support organization for cross-dressers and transgender people. Bart promised there would be lots of potential clients for me there. He said, "Don't be scared. Don't be judgmental. Treat them like you would anybody else."

This was back in 1990, when I was in my early thirties. The circumstances of my life to that point had definitely predisposed me to be open minded and accepting. Bart introduced me to many people that first evening, including Vernon, the man who owned the building where the meeting was taking place. Vernon was a full-time cross-dresser who made his living teaching square dancing. He also owned a clothing store located on the first floor of the same building, which was very convenient for folks who weren't ready to go out to the mall to do their shopping.

Bart also introduced me to Merissa Lynn, the editor of *Tapestry* magazine and the founder of the International Foundation for Gender Education (IFGE), of which the Tiffany Club was a component. Right away Merissa suggested I write an article about skin care for the magazine, because hair removal and skin care go hand in hand and are very important to people making gender transitions. The shop where the magazine was being produced was in the same building too, on the second floor, and Merissa offered to give me a tour. There were lots of people busy in there that evening, clicking away on keyboards and looking at cover-design layouts. Merissa sat me down in a chair in her office to further discuss what she wanted me to write. I didn't see myself as a writer, but I didn't want to turn down the opportunity either.

My Writing Career Begins

I went home and poured everything I knew about skin care into the first draft of my first article. I took it in to show Merissa a few days later. She read it, and, to my horror, she ripped it up. She said, "I don't want this!"

I was stunned. I started to cry.

"This isn't how you write!" she continued. "This sounds like a textbook. Tell me real stories about real people with real skin problems. Tell me what you know from experience, not from what you studied in school."

My inclination was to tell her nothing, other than that I wasn't interested in working with her after all. But I took a minute to think it over and decided that would be a mistake. She was offering me an opportunity to reach many potential clients, people I didn't understand yet but who had been gracious and kind to me at the meeting I had attended with Bart.

She opened her drawer and took out a tape recorder. She said, "Take this and start talking. I'll type it up later." So I pulled myself together and told her a story about a man who had the beginnings of folliculitis barbae, a rare but serious bacterial infection of the deeper layers of the skin and subcutaneous tissues. This man was a cross-dressing pilot in the military. He had come to my office in full uniform. He was handsome, gorgeous—except for his skin problem. When I inquired, he told me he had been shaving with an electric shaver, and he admitted that he didn't regularly take the time to clean it. Nor did he take the time to wash his face properly after he shaved. Next appointment I had him bring in the shaver and show me. I explained that his pores were absorbing the debris left in the shaver between shaves. I took the shaver apart and showed him how to clean it properly with alcohol and a little brush to get out even the tiniest fragments of hair and shaving gunk. When it was clean, I let it vibrate for a while in case there was anything left in there. In the meantime, I gave him a crash course on how to wash his face and what products to use to help get rid of his infection. He came back one more time, to show me how well his skin had cleared. His infection was gone. Merissa loved it.

After a while I knew what Merissa wanted from me, and we didn't need the tape recorder anymore to coax it out. Many of the people from the transgender community were afraid to go to the doctor when they had a skin concern because they didn't want to admit that the problem had come about as a result of their own efforts to get rid of unwanted hair somewhere on their body. But they began to see my name over and over in the magazine, and some of them sensed that they could trust me. That was what Merissa had intended; she wanted me to take care of her people.

There was nothing else like *Tapestry* magazine at the time. If you didn't subscribe by mail you could get it at the "Out of Town News" newsstand in the middle of Harvard Square. The IFGE itself hadn't been around all that long. Not only was *Tapestry* full of important information for readers, but there was a personal section where people could meet and make new friends. There were so many people out there in the world who had known since childhood that the gender they presented was not the same as the one they knew themselves to be within, but who could they tell? Where could they go with that kind of story? Back then most of them wouldn't have had the language to express what they were feeling even if they wanted to talk about it. Now, finally, thanks to the IFGE, some were learning they were not alone in the world. And those who wanted to close the gap between who they were and how they presented had information on where to go to find the services they would need to do so.

Merissa and I eventually became good friends. She finished her electrolysis with me before her SRS in 1991, and in the late 1990s, at a difficult time in my career, Merissa Lynn helped me save my business, referring several clients from the IFGE. I continued to write articles for *Tapestry* magazine and became a regular contributor to the conversation on skin care and hair removal for transitioning individuals.

This book was written to help not only people who are considering transitioning but also those who want to better understand people who have transitioned or are thinking about it, and even those who are simply curious. I have tried to answer both the medical and psychological questions that come up before, during, and after transition. My data is informed by both my wonderful, generous clients and the medical community we work with. Several of my clients allowed me to interview them so that their stories could be included. I am grateful that each of them trusted me enough to participate. Each story is different, and each story is true. I know you will enjoy them.

A note on terminology: The term used for physical transition surgery throughout this book is "sex reassignment surgery (SRS)."

However, medical professionals and transgender people use various terms. Dr. Marci Bowers uses the term genital reassignment surgery. Other terms in use include but are not limited to gender reassignment surgery, gender affirming surgery, gender confirming surgery, and bottom surgery.

This book is dedicated to tolerance, for all people everywhere but especially for transgender people. If you are looking for an excuse to open your heart to transgender individuals, you can find one. But hopefully once you've read these pages, your acceptance will be automatic.

The information written in this book should not be used in any way to replace proper health-care provider advice, direction, prescription, and consultation.

Acknowledgments

I had just finished working on two other books, a memoir and a children's book, when I realized that the world was changing. People who had never given a single thought to their transgender brothers and sisters were beginning to become aware of their existence and wanted to know more about them. Exhausted from years of satisfying my need to write while also running a busy company, I didn't think I had the energy to start yet a third writing project. Yet I had to acknowledge that I was perfectly qualified for this one. I worked with members of the transgender community, I knew many of the therapists and doctors who would help them attain their goals, and I was deeply inspired by all of them. Still, in the end, it was the encouragement that I received from the amazing, wonderful, and creative people I have been so fortunate to find in my life that made this book a reality. Thank you, one and all.

Thanks to my sweet husband, Greg, whose everlasting love, patience, and wonderful sense of humor always endure throughout these book journeys. He understands how important my writing life is to me and continues to encourage and support me. He lets me be me! I couldn't have completed this project without him. Greg, I love you more than you'll ever know.

Thanks to my beloved sister Lois, who never lost interest in this project, even while she had so many dire concerns of her own to deal with. Thanks to Scottie, Lois's transgender, cross-dressing husband, who took full-time care of my terminally ill sister. The joy, laughter, and health-care support Scottie brought to Lois was a blessing for both of us. Her memory will live on in those of us who loved her best.

Thanks to my mother, Jean, my father, Joe, my stepfather, Frankie, and my younger sister, Jodi, all of whom have passed on but each of whom taught me everything I know about unconditional love, loyalty, dedication, and compassion. Not a day goes by that I do not think of them and reflect on the love and happiness they brought into my life. My mother especially seemed to me to be a kind of magician when I was growing up because she knew so much and could juggle so many tasks at a time. In fact, my mother was an electrologist too. I've learned to love to be busy, as she did; I've learned to love learning, and over the years I've followed in her footsteps and acquired licenses and certifications in a multitude of skills.

I also owe thanks for love and support to my brother, Stephen, and other family members.

I am grateful to Fenway Health for their high-quality health care, research, education, and advocacy for the transgender community. Likewise, I am grateful for the Center for Transgender Medicine and Surgery at Boston Medical Center, which follows the WPATH (World Professional Association for Transgender Health) Standards of Care and the Endocrine Society Guidelines for the care of transgender patients. Without the wonderful health-care networks and medical staffs here in the Boston area and throughout the state, the tendencies we are seeing from more and more state governments to take stock of the needs of their transgender communities might not have begun. I also want to salute some of the amazing doctors I have come to know, including Drs. Toby Meltzer, Marci Bowers, Kathy Rumer, Mark Zukowski, Jeffrey Spiegel, and others, for their dedication to the transgender community.

Thanks to my fabulous friends, who always encourage and inspire me, not only with their kind words but also with their unconditional love.

Thanks to my staff at A&A. You all held down the fort with grace and ease whenever I had to turn in the other direction to respond to the needs of this book project (and previous ones).

Thanks to Joan Schweighardt, my smart, hardworking, and dedicated editor and research assistant. I am fortunate to have worked with you over the years. You paved the way for me to achieve my goals and helped make my work shine.

Thank you to the many talented and conscientious people at Brown Books Publishing Group. Brown published my children's book, but a book of profiles of transgender people is a little bit different than a book about adopting kittens, and I didn't want to work with a publisher who would be in any way ungracious regarding this book's subject matter. In fact, Brown was the opposite. Everyone there let me know right away that they loved the idea for this book and would be honored to be part of its journey toward publication.

In particular, thanks to Sherry LeVine, the gatekeeper at Brown, a woman whose good humor and willingness to listen and help is always apparent. Thanks to Katlin Stewart, project coordinator, for overseeing all aspects of this project, for addressing and answering all of my many questions and requests, and for keeping me motivated, inspired, focused, and dedicated. Thanks to Hallie Raymond, not only for her editing mastery but for her engagement in the subject matter and her great suggestions for generating a format that would balance the many components this book features.

Thank you to the many people who read and critiqued early drafts (or parts thereof) of this book and offered ideas for improvements. I greatly appreciate your time, patience, and invaluable input.

Thank you to Diane Ellaborn, LICSW, for her years of dedication as a gender specialist and for her ability to recognize each individual's differences as well as the unique strengths that would allow them to build a successful and satisfying life. Diane is an expert in the field of gender dysphoria. She educates staff and employees in the workplace, she delivers lectures, and she supports yearly workshops and staff at First Event conferences. And still she has time to be interested in the work of her colleagues and to provide useful information to them when she can. Diane added to my Recommended Reading list in these pages by providing some general titles as well as appropriate titles for young adults.

Finally, last but hardly least, thanks to all the people who shared their stories in these pages. How fortunate I have been to get to know each and every one of you! Your bravery and honesty are invaluable and inspirational. Thank you from the bottom of my heart for putting your full trust and confidence in me. Each of your stories provides a pathway into your heart, and each path is unique. You divulged your obstacles, revealed your sorrows, and shared your joys. I am humbled and grateful and blessed to have had the chance to accompany you on your journeys.

And thanks also to my many clients from within the transgender community here in the Boston metro area and throughout the United States. While some of you were not inclined to participate in this book, many of you generously answered my questions, and all of you encouraged me to write the book and cheered me on in times when the project overwhelmed me.

You all hold a special place in my heart. Thank you so much!

FAQs

While I'm not an academic scholar on transgender issues, because I work so closely with transgender individuals (and their therapists, endocrinologists, and various surgeons) and because I am an asker of questions, a listener to answers, and a relentless researcher, I am confident enough to consider myself knowledgeable on the subject. Alongside the stories of individuals who have transitioned, this book will include some sections providing information I have learned over the years, in the hopes that it will help others that may be looking for answers. Let's start with the basics.

FAQ: What causes gender dysphoria?

There are several theories out there, the most popular of which is that fetal chromosome abnormalities are responsible. Another theory is that gender identity disorder is the result of millions of women having taken a man-made form of estrogen called diethylstilbestrol (DES) to help prevent miscarriages during pregnancy between 1938 and 1971. These women, the theory goes, who inadvertently also put themselves at risk for vaginal, cervical, and breast cancer, may have passed the DES on to their sons, who may have grown up to have gender identity disorder as a result. At a now defunct "Be-All" conference in Chicago four or five years ago, a presenting doctor asked the audience how many of them thought their mothers might have been affected by DES while pregnant with them. Most of the people in the room raised their hands. There are other theories, but almost all medical professionals agree that gender dysphoria is biological. It does not constitute mental illness. In fact, many transgender people who were on antidepressants before transitioning get off them after they complete SRS and/or FFS (facial feminizing surgery). They stay on hormone therapy for life with regular monitoring through their primary care physician and their endocrinologist and sometimes their therapist too. Because they are on a schedule to constantly monitor blood levels and medications, they can be more health conscious (and therefore often healthier) than some nontransgender people.

From Linda's Office

Basically there are two ways to remove hair permanently from your face and/or body—electrolysis and laser.

Electrolysis is performed with a tool called an epilator. Because electrolysis was around long before laser hair removal, many people think that the laser has now replaced electrolysis, but in fact that is not the case. Electrolysis still plays an important part in hair removal for most people.

Electrolysis removes hairs by pulling them out, more or less one at a time, via insertion of a very fine probe (and its accompanying tiny electrical charge) into the hair follicles. When performed by an experienced technician, this means that the growth center of the hair is usually damaged, and the chances of the hair being permanently removed are enough to justify the FDA's "permanent removal" sign-off. The slight stinging and discomfort most people experience with electrolysis can be addressed with a skin cream, and generally by the next day any soreness and redness is gone.

The great thing about electrolysis is that it can be used to remove virtually anyone's hair. It doesn't matter what color or texture your hair is or what color your skin is. Nor does it matter how old you are. The downside of electrolysis is that it can take quite a long time, especially if you are interested in removing hair from your entire body.

FAQ: Where do psychiatrists and psychologists weigh in on transgender issues?

According to the American Psychological Association, "There is no single explanation for why some people are transgender. The diversity of transgender expression and experiences argues against any simple or unitary explanation. Many experts believe that biological factors such as genetic influences and prenatal hormone levels, early experiences, and experiences later in adolescence or adulthood may all contribute to the development of transgender identities." Then again, there are those who continue to argue otherwise. Dr. Paul R. McHugh, the former psychiatrist-in-chief for Johns Hopkins Hospital and its current Distinguished Service Professor of Psychiatry, states that transgenderism is a mental disorder that "merits treatment" and that people who promote sex reassignment surgery are collaborating with and promoting a mental disorder. As long as there are still people like Dr. McHugh around, there is work to be done to change attitudes and open minds.

FAQ: What is the difference between gender assignment, gender identification, and gender expression?

Gender assignment is what is recorded on a baby's birth certificate—male or female. Gender identity occurs later—usually, as we can see in these pages, in early childhood—and it may not always coincide with what was written on the birth certificate. A girl might identify as a boy, or a boy might identify as a girl. But in reality it's not even that simple, because there can be degrees of identification, so that, for instance, a child assigned a male identity at birth may later feel himself to be half female.

Gender expression is of course how one chooses to present oneself. Someone assigned to be male at birth may identify as a female but still choose to express "herself" as male in order not to

3

stand out or bring affliction into her life. When we say someone is trans female, we are noting that the person is moving toward an expression of a gender that differs from the one assigned at birth. As noted elsewhere, gender identification and gender expression are unrelated to sexual orientation. Trans people can be heterosexual, gay, lesbian, bisexual, or asexual—or combinations thereof, just like anyone else.

FAQ: Are there federal laws to protect the rights of LGBT individuals?

As of this writing, there are state laws in some states, and I'm proud to say that my state, Massachusetts, is one of the leaders of the pack. But until there are federal laws, across-the-board protections for LGBT people cannot be assumed. There are, however, various organizations working toward this goal. One of them is the Movement Advancement Project (MAP), which defines itself as follows:

> *"Founded in 2006, the Movement Advancement Project is an independent think tank that provides rigorous research, insight and analysis that help speed equality for lesbian, gay, bisexual and transgender (LGBT) people. MAP's work is focused on three primary areas: Policy & Issue Analysis; LGBT Movement Overviews; Effective Messaging."*

FAQ: Is it really possible to adjust the body to the mind?

Yes, of course. That's what this book is about. All the stories you will find in these pages are about people who made the choice to adjust their bodies to suit their minds. For some of these individuals, it is enough to start dressing and styling in accordance with the gender with which they identify. For others, nothing but a full transition will do.

Either way, the best place to start is with a health-care provider, physician, psychiatrist, psychologist, or gender therapist who can officially diagnose the individual's gender dysphoria and recommend a treatment plan. Once the diagnosis has been made, a referral will be made to an endocrinologist for hormone therapy.

Surgical therapy should begin with inquiry. There are many things for an individual to consider beyond whether or not they want the outcome that SRS promises. Can they afford it? This is a huge consideration for many people. Will their insurance pay any part of the tab, or will they be responsible for all of it? Is their general health good enough to withstand surgery? If they are unhealthy, or perhaps obese, they may want to work on achieving a better physical condition before they move forward. Many doctors recommend patients stop smoking before beginning hormone replacement therapy (HRT), because smoking may increase the risks, and most SRS surgeons will refuse to work on anyone who is sickly or significantly overweight. And what about age? Doctors prefer the clients be at least eighteen years old. The several young clients I've worked with could hardly wait. We've talked about people in their seventies who have undergone SRS, but we have to assume they were in relatively good health, maybe "young" for their age. What about people who are "old" for their age? Or people who are really old, like maybe in their nineties? And some people may just not be able to handle the stress of surgery, which is—let's face it—a very threatening prospect. And even when all the ducks are lined up neat and tidy in a row and the individual has decided to move forward, they will have to spend a period of time living full time in the gender with which they identify. They may be alarmed to find that there are days when the idea of SRS seems so immense that it doesn't make sense anymore. That's normal; it means they are really considering how serious their undertaking is. It's called cold feet, and we all know that just about everyone experiences cold feet before taking on any major life change.

If you would like more information on what it means to be transgender, please take a look at the resources for further reading provided at the back of this book.

From Linda's Office

Zoë was about forty years old when she first came to us. She had hoped to tackle her hair growth aggressively but had already spent two hundred hours visiting an out-of-state hair removal facility, exclusively for electrolysis, before we ever saw her. We worked with her for another one hundred hours, for a three-hundred-hour total.

Zoë spent approximately $21,000 for the first two hundred hours at the out-of-state facility. She spent another $10,000 with us, $8,500 for her facial hair removal and the other $1,500 for her body. Of the $31,000 she spent overall between both locations, most of it was spent on electrolysis for her face. This was because laser didn't work for her. Her light-colored hair was coarse, but more importantly, her follicles happened to be very deep. In fact, she had what we in the business call "distorted" hairs, which are hairs in which the tough base of the hair is not straight but twisted against the follicle wall, almost as if there is a little hook on the end. This condition can be caused by plucking or tweezing hair over long periods of time. But even regular shaving can "distort" hair when the hair is as coarse as Zoë's was.

Because Zoë lived four hours away from our office, she did four-hour visits, making for very long days for her. In spite of her hope to attack her hair aggressively, her tough, coarse hair fought back, requiring Zoë to spend a total of seven years getting rid of her unwanted hair.

Stories of Transition

Grace

Grace made the decision to transition in 2010, at the age of sixty-three. She had been married between 1976 and 2001 and couldn't even bring herself to say words like "transsexual" or "transgender" before her decision.

Grace had been an engineer all her life. In her most recent position, she had been a highly visible, senior-level program manager working in a large company on a campus shared by over one thousand people. When she was ready to transition, she went directly to the president of the company and explained that after the four-week leave of absence suggested for her facial surgery and recovery, she would be returning to work as a woman. The president asked why she was coming to him with that information; the company had an antidiscrimination policy. Grace told him that support starts from the top down. If anybody came to him with a complaint about her, he had to be aware and ready to defend her rights. Then she went to her peers, and to her surprise she found that they were all supportive. While she was away for her surgery, her therapist, Diane Ellaborn, came in and did two training sessions with two hundred or so people at the company to further instruct them on what to expect and how they could best show their support when Grace returned.

Over the course of Grace's engineering career, there was an average of one occasion per decade where she would find herself laid off. For this reason she had decided back in 2004 to go back to school and get a backup degree, an MA in counseling psychology.

By the time of her transition, she had received her degree and was working at a substance abuse clinic a couple of nights a week facilitating drunk driver groups. As she did not feel it would be helpful for clients who knew her as a man to suddenly see her as a woman, she terminated her individual clients, left the clinic for three months, and started fresh with new clients posttransition.

From 2008 to 2013, Grace worked days in the tech world and a few nights each week as a clinician. Thereafter she left her tech job and worked solely as a counselor. She hadn't known she would make the transition back when she started working toward her second degree; at that time she had only been thinking that it would be a good idea to have a plan in place to cope with the shifts and bumps that went on in the engineering world. But looking back, she now believes that she was led to study therapy, perhaps by the universe, because the timing was too perfect. This and other instances of serendipity have helped her to trust herself and her instincts.

Grace is a gentle therapist, but she is the first to admit that she was not that likeable back when she lived as a man. She had an A-type personality when she worked in engineering, and while she was not a large person, she would use a large voice and her acute mental skills to intimidate others when she felt it would serve her purpose. Like many transgender women, she had been hypermasculine as a boy. It was her way of protecting herself and making sure no one ever learned her secret. In fact, she was a bully for a while when she was a kid—until she learned to use her tongue instead of her fists. Except for her aggressive tendencies, she appeared balanced as a male. No one would have ever guessed she was a mess inside.

Grace was about eight or nine when her confusion first surfaced. By then she knew that her inclinations would not be tolerated, and thus she learned to be ashamed of her own thoughts. She would be a wreck when she tried on her mother's clothes when she was home alone. Part of her mind would be marveling at how right, how relaxed she was wearing female garments. The other part would be listening for any tiny sound that might indicate that her mother was coming back early and she might get caught.

She never did get caught, but an accordion teacher who wasn't happy with her musical skills would sometimes say to her, "You're such a girl," or, "You're such a sissy." Perhaps they were names he called all his male students, but it was also possible that he was seeing something in Grace that she didn't want anyone to see. She couldn't take the chance. She quit her accordion studies. She kept her acquaintances at arm's length for the same reason. What could be worse as a kid than to be called "queer" or labeled "effeminate"? She was lonely a lot of the time. But she was always busy in her head. She didn't know how she fit in. She was attracted to females, but she felt female. There was no information anywhere. The only relief came from the television, which allowed her to numb out and forget herself for a while.

Grace got married and had children. She'd learned how to sew when she was younger, and she often made clothes that were ostensibly for her wife. But they were more or less the same size, and when her wife and kids were out of the house she would wear them, along with other garments belonging to her wife. Things were no different than when she had been a kid. Half of her mind experienced the genuine relaxation that comes when you glimpse internal authenticity, while the other half was questioning every sound.

Once, when Grace was younger, a neighbor came to the door, and when Grace, who was dressed, didn't answer, she shouted, "I know you're in there!" The neighbor needed something, apparently, but there was no way Grace could help her at that moment. It was an agonizing experience. But the compulsion to dress remained stronger than the fear of being found out.

"I know you're in there" could have been Grace's mantra. Because she was smart and observant and cautious, she was able to live a life of denial for many years. But in her third year of her graduate school program, she signed up for a course on counseling in the LGBT community, and the first day of class, the students were encouraged to say why they were there. As Grace waited for her turn to speak, she knew she was about to come out. And she did; she told the others that she had been wrestling with gender issues all her life. No one questioned her about the details. But later in the semester she did a presentation on the movement from male to female. A cartoon of an elephant in the room was her prop. She said to the class, "I'm this elephant. I'm transgender." She made friends with four people that semester—four females who wanted to go out with her as Grace and help her move along on her journey. Until that time she would dress in her apartment, but never outside of it.

After the presentation, she knew she had to find community, and she forced herself to join the Tiffany Club. She had known about them for years. She had "stalked" them on the internet, looking at the people in the various photos and wondering how they managed to do what they did. The theme at the Tiffany Club was "you are not alone." Grace needed not to feel alone anymore—and now she isn't.

Call Me Whatever You Want

Grace continued to work as a therapist until February 2015, when she decided to devote all her time to writing, training, and speaking. When she first started facilitating Driver Alcohol Education (DAE) classes, she would explain that they were in denial about their drinking or drugging problems, and then she would go home and cry, because she was in denial herself. Now she doesn't do that anymore.

Grace has also created a consulting company called Gender Variance Education and Training. This is another way that she has found to do her part to foster a more positive and accepting society for other people like herself. Grace goes into schools and corporations to teach people about the need to be authentic in their lives. For her, the issue was gender, but there are many people out there struggling with who they are on the inside, people who feel they must hold themselves back from living their truth. She has presented on different transgender and relationship topics in a variety of settings both within and outside of the gender-variant community. She teaches that gender identification and sexual orientation have nothing to do with each other. There is a whole spectrum of gender variance. Gender is about continuity. Most believe it is binary; one is either male or female. But it's actually very fluid. The way one feels and the way one presents oneself may be aligned sometimes, but not always.

In addition to her training programs, Grace is an active leader in the local New England LGBT community. She is a board member for the Tiffany Club and a coleader of the annual First Event conferences. Grace has multiple published titles. Her first book, entitled *No! Maybe? Yes! Living My Truth* (a memoir, but also including essays on love, forgiveness, relationships and authenticity, and life transitions), was published in January 2015. She also writes a weekly column for the *Huffington Post* called My Transgender Life and is a regular speaker for a variety of organizations. (More information about her work is available at www.GraceAnneStevens.com.)

Grace feels blessed that no one in her family (which includes three adult children and one grandchild) abandoned her when she transitioned. Wondering if they might had been her greatest concern. If they had, though, it would have been their own journey, and she would have only been able to hope it ultimately led them to a place of compassion and acceptance.

Not only were her children accepting but her ex-wife was supportive with the kids too. She reminded the kids, "You don't abandon family." Grace feels very fortunate, because many people in the transgender community have problems with this. Her two older children call her Grace. The youngest still calls her Dad. He says that he knew her for twenty-five years as Dad, and he can't know her another way now. Grace says that's fine. She *is* still a dad. She certainly does not think of herself as anyone's mother. She transitioned her gender in 2011. She's not trying to rewrite history. Her children love her; she knows that; they can call her whatever they want.

Grace starts and ends each day with gratitude. She is happy to be on her journey, living her life. The day she came home from her facial surgery, the voices in her head, which she had been hearing almost all her life, stopped chattering. It wasn't about the surgery itself. Surgery is a level of detail. Some people don't want any surgery. But for Grace, the surgery was emblematic of her commitment. Afterward she knew she was Grace; she knew she was doing the right thing.

Grace has no secrets now. She is baring her soul to friends and to audiences during presentations and to even larger crowds through her book. She became an engineer because she was a geeky kid who was good at science and math—and she realized facts and numbers could help her distance herself from people and emotions. As she learned to accept her true self and live honestly and authentically, she realized that her gender was not the only thing in her life that transitioned. Now she has become a storyteller and a role model. She didn't plan for it; it has come about as a result of her being herself.

From Linda's Office

Grace, who started hair removal at age sixty-two, had 180 hours of electrolysis and 28 hours of laser, for both her face and body. She was with us for six years, though we did the bulk of the work in the first four. She spent about $8,000 in total for her treatments.

Rikki

Rikki started drumming in 1965. Her instructor was Boston Pops classical percussionist Warren Myers, and her lessons included orchestral studies, jazz, and Latin beats. She got her first real drum kit in 1966 (as opposed to the toy kits her parents bought her after her obsession was triggered by kid drummers starring on the *Mickey Mouse Club*) and started playing in garage bands. In 1973, she began attending Berklee College of Music, where she added composition to her repertoire.

In 1978, Rikki moved to Cape Cod and joined Travis & Shook, the band opening for famed comedian / social critic George Carlin at that time. After two years together, the band took on a new name, the Incredible Casuals, and it has been called that ever since. They did some covers, but they also wrote hundreds of their own tunes and were often described as "the Beach Boys meet the Who." In addition to playing a variety of venues, the Incredible Casuals became a Sunday-and-summer fixture at the Beachcomber of Wellfleet on the Cape. Over the years they put out some records, and the music media picked up on them. They were reviewed in *Rolling Stone*. And an article in *People* magazine featured a photo of Rikki, then known by another name (and a different gender). Thirteen years flew by. Rikki loved working with the Incredible Casuals. She loved that they were finally getting national attention. And she loved that she was making more money that she'd ever made before in her life. Then the bottom fell out.

Rikki's eight-year marriage had recently come to an end. She'd told her wife on their first date that on the inside she was a woman, but her wife, a great fan of punk rock, saw Rikki's declaration as some version of male musician behavior. When she realized that wasn't what was going on, problems began.

With her marriage behind her (there hadn't been any children), Rikki went into therapy. Her therapist, a lesbian who did presentations at transgender conferences and who really understood the whole transgender thing, saw what had to happen right away. Rikki went in as a boy to that first appointment. The therapist had her out and presenting as herself a week later. Thereafter she went to an endocrinologist and got on hormones.

The people in her life were shocked. Some of them felt like they had been duped all this time. Others felt she was making a big mistake and that she should try harder to live with what she had, so to speak. Her mother was shocked, but only for about twenty seconds, Rikki says. Not only were her parents very liberal, but her mom had a master's in early childhood education; she'd given Rikki the space to figure it out for herself as a kid; she'd urged her into therapy, but she'd never yelled at her or denigrated her feelings. As for the Incredible Casuals, however, that was another story. It would take them years to come around. It wasn't that they minded so much what Rikki did with her life as it was that they were anxious about fan reaction.

The band tolerated her for a while, as long as she agreed not to go on stage dressed as a woman. Her therapy sessions were a few hours away in Boston. When they had Boston-area gigs, they would meet up with Rikki in a parking lot. Once in the van with the boys, she had to change out of her girl clothes and remove her makeup quickly before they reached their venue. It was clear they were disgusted by her. It was humiliating. And then they fired her some months later anyway.

Rikki was devastated. For the first full year, when she wasn't going to therapy sessions or to the depression clinic at Mass General, she stayed in bed and cried. Her income dropped to zero overnight, another huge problem. Reluctantly, she sought out social services and got on SSI (Supplemental Security Income) to keep from starving.

The first person to come forward and befriend her again was a musician named Bruce Maclean, who used the stage name Link Montana. He had a small recording studio, and he got her busy recording with him. They also did some gigs together. It was a start. Then a few years later, in 1994, she met Ryan Landry, who was well known in Provincetown, mostly for his drag performances. He wanted to start a rock band, and Rikki was able to help him put it together. He didn't mind at all that Rikki was transgender. He wanted to play to the LGBT community in Provincetown, and everyone else as well. Rikki knew a guitarist who was totally straight but a great performer. She brought him on board, and Ryan brought on some others, and voilà, Space Pussy was born.

No one knew how Space Pussy would be received. The gay community in Provincetown, Rikki says, liked cabaret and disco. Rock performances were intimidating; rock was where you went when you wanted to get beat up. But Ryan was the kind of guy you could present to a straight world or a "less than." Besides being really handsome, he had great moves, and people liked to watch him. And he and Rikki had gathered together some of the most talented musicians around.

Word spread. Their first performance was totally packed—with both straight and LGBT locals. The band had been rehearsing with the amps turned down low. But Rikki told the guitarist to crank his up that first night, and she cranked hers up too, and the band played some ass-kicking rock 'n' roll to an exuberant, totally-blown-away full house that couldn't get enough of them.

The band gained popularity. There were labels interested. But there were also some problems with management, and after a time Rikki took a step back from her work with them. Around the same time, Chandler Travis from the Incredible Casuals showed up again in her life. It had been nine years since Rikki had been fired from the band, and he still hadn't found a drummer to replace her. The Incredible Casuals was a loud rock band. Now Chandler wanted to go quieter, to do some exploratory work, original music incorporating jazz, African music, and bossa nova. His new band would be called the Chandler Travis Philharmonic. He wanted Rikki to be part of it.

As for the rest of the Incredible Casuals, they were still playing, but they would not be playing with the new band. Chandler was taking on new musicians to go with the new sound he was hoping to produce. The consensus among the new guys regarding Rikki's transgenderism was basically, "Who gives a fuck?" To them, the only thing that mattered was exceptional musicianship, and *that*, everyone agreed, Rikki had in spades.

In the end, even the remaining Incredible Casuals acquiesced and invited Rikki to rejoin the group. But by then they'd been in existence for thirty-something years, and it turned out to be nearly time to call it quits anyway.

Now and Then

As of this writing, Rikki still plays with the Chandler Travis Philharmonic, and she plays with other bands as well. Since the '70s she has been singled out for her part in the New England underground music scene. Her life in the spotlight has kept her from experiencing at least some of the introversion that afflicts some transgender women once they've come out. "We're all human beings, and pretty much the same things push our buttons," she says matter-of-factly. "In the end, we just need to be kind and understanding toward one another."

Rikki attributes her ease with herself to the fact that she is able to focus inwardly, on her music, rather than pay too much attention to what is going on around her. But it wasn't always that way. She knew there was something different about her from as early as age four. She recalls a babysitter once urging her to go off and play with a group of boys whose behavior she could tell even from across the street was rowdy and aggressive. Reluctantly, she succumbed to the sitter's coaxing and joined them. But the boys got that she was different right away and singled her out for abuse. That was the first of many instances of abuse that Rikki would endure as she entered elementary school.

Rikki grew up thinking that she was probably just more "fucked up" than other people. She knew she was bisexual, so her confusion wasn't really related to her sexual preferences. It had more to do with sexual identity. In fact, it had everything to do with her sexual identity.

From Linda's Office

Rikki has spent five years (2011 to 2016) and a total of $15,015 on hair removal. She underwent her first two hundred hours of electrolysis on her face and neck at a hair removal facility local to her residence over a period of two years and at a cost of about $7,000. Thereafter, she came to our office wanting a consultation and second opinion on her progress. She underwent another forty-two hours with us, over a period of three years and at a total cost of $8,015–$3,740 for electrolysis and $4,275 for facial and full-body laser work.

It is not unusual for the hair removal process to take this long. The heavier, darker hairs are the first to be removed, and the very finest hairs are last. The people who don't mind very fine hairs remaining may need less time to complete the process. In some cases hair removal can take a lifetime, because of lack of money, lack of convenience to hair-removal services, and other circumstances. Or some people may choose to undergo temporary hair-removal methods, such as shaving, tweezing, plucking or waxing or chemical treatments, etc. As previously noted, some of these temporary methods can wreak havoc, causing irritation or ingrown hairs on the skin. It's important to keep your skin clean and to clean the tools you use on it regularly.

Rikki's skin looks amazing now: smooth and completely natural.

Finding Peace

Rikki is sixty years old now. Like so many others in Massachusetts, she is ecstatic about the new MassHealth regulations instituted by Governor Deval Patrick that will make it possible for low-income residents who are transgender to undergo hormone therapy and gender reassignment surgery (GRS). In large part, these regulations have come about because of Rikki. With the backing of her lawyers and some well-timed media attention, including a prominent article in the *Boston Globe*, she began a high-profile suit against MassHealth some time prior to the governor's proclamation.

Nevertheless, there is still a long ways to go to ensure that the MassHealth payments toward various treatments are consistent with the cost of the treatments and not simply a token effort meant to satisfy the regulations. In the meantime, the governor has recommended changes to the Group Insurance Commission, which provides coverage for many state and municipal employees and their families. It does look likely that SRS will eventually be available for all who want it.

Other states are quickly coming to the same conclusion, perhaps motivated by a 2013 resolution put out by the American Medical Association. The AMA now supports full equality for transgender and gender-variant people and upholds their right to legal and social recognition and medically necessary treatments (including those required for gender transition), and it has called on public and private insurers to cover these treatments.

After years of having to keep their sexual identities a secret, these changes should result in a rush of closet doors being thrown open. The problem is that there are an insufficient number of doctors trained to perform sex reassignment surgery. Still, Rikki and others can rest assured that inner peace is on the horizon.

More Light on the Horizon

Rikki had a gig in Pennsylvania some years ago, and afterward the musicians were farmed out to the homes of a handful of people who were willing to put them up for the night. Rikki really liked the couple who had taken her in. They talked that night, and they talked again the morning. They had never met a transgender woman before, and they were exceedingly interested and asked a lot of good questions.

The woman, who was a well-known journalist, began a project after meeting Rikki. She hoped to follow Rikki through some portion of her future, including her sex reassignment surgery, and create a documentary so that the rest of the world can see what she sees when she looks at Rikki—a warm, intelligent, talented woman who is as deserving of as full a life as anyone else on the planet.

Rikki's advocacy for her own rights and the rights of others continued to have an impact—she has been interviewed for at least two different newspaper articles—but getting her SRS took some time.

Having set out to require MassHealth to pay for her surgery, Rikki eventually secured a hearing with MassHealth, and they promised their decision would follow. But then they asked for extra time, as they hoped to be able to submit more evidence to the court officer deciding the case. But the evidence never came, apparently, and neither did a final decision.

Just when it appeared they'd hit a wall, Rikki's lawyers at GLAAD received a call from MassHealth saying they'd be willing to pay for Rikki's surgery if Rikki dropped charges against them. Considering all MassHealth's posturing, Rikki's lawyers were suspicious at first. They thought there must be some kind of a catch. They debated the possibilities and decided the offer was legitimate. Rikki and her team accepted their offer.

The motivations for the MassHealth turnaround were very interesting. MassHealth first called Rikki's lawyer at GLAAD on June 13, 2014, asking to resolve the case out of court. Rikki and GLAAD accepted their offer three days later, on June 17. Three days after that, on June 20, then-governor Deval Patrick announced that MassHealth would be making changes to their policy regulations to include coverage for transgender individuals. There had been a widely publicized case prior to Rikki's. A convicted murderer diagnosed with gender identity disorder was also suing the state for refusing to pay for his sex reassignment surgery. Conservative newsmakers throughout the state (and nationally) were using his petition to suggest that the murderer, Robert/Michelle Kosilek, was the true face of transgenderism. They were enraged that the courts seemed to be taking Kosilek's side on the issue.

Deval Patrick needed someone else to step up and become the first transgender person in the state to receive the green light from MassHealth insurance coverage for sex reassignment surgery. With Rikki's case also waiting in the wings, the timing was right for Deval to make his announcement.

Rikki is the first to admit that her own motives were self-serving when she first began the long process of writing letters to politicians and legal organizations that would lead her to Jennifer Levi, her lawyer at GLAAD. But as time goes on, she sees that her case has had the power to reshape the way Medicaid-affiliated insurance companies everywhere deal with transgender issues. She was more than willing to take on the job of being spokesperson for transgender individuals seeking medical care appropriate to their needs and rights. Her case provided Deval Patrick with the opening he needed, and he jumped for it. Rikki was the first person in Massachusetts to undergo sex reassignment surgery through her Medicaid insurance carrier. She had waited for the surgery her entire life. For her courage and her persistence, the First Parish Brewster Unitarian Universalist Church in Brewster, Massachusetts, presented Rikki with the Skip Warren Award, honoring transgender women making a difference.

That should have been the end of Rikki's transition surgery, but there were still mounds of red tape blocking her from her surgery. When Deval Patrick made his announcement regarding MassHealth policy changes, it became necessary for policy makers to rewrite regulations, which alone took about six months. The next wall Rikki hit had to do with a problem that is common to all people covered under Medicaid or Medicare policies: she had to find a doctor who would take her insurance, and since there are not enough SRS doctors to begin with, this was a virtually impossible task. The only doctor willing to work with her had some very bad reviews for his work.

Rikki decided to contact a well-known SRS surgeon. The doctor's assistant told Rikki the doctor didn't accept Medicaid either, but Rikki went on to tell the story of her long and tedious engagement with MassHealth, and in the end, the assistant agreed to pass the information on the doctor. Rikki followed up by sending the doctor's office a few of the many articles that had been written about her by then. Not long after, Rikki received notice from the doctor's assistant: the doctor was impressed with Rikki's achievements and would love to do her surgery pro bono.

But complications persisted even then. While the doctor was willing to offer services for free, there were still the costs of the assisting staff, the anesthesiologist, and the hospital itself. Rikki had to travel for the surgery. She would need to be hospitalized for some days and then stay in a hotel afterward until she had had her follow-up appointments and was deemed sufficiently recovered to fly home. The doctor had not wanted any association with MassHealth, because the doctor did not want to set a precedent of accepting payment through Medicaid. But in the end the doctor was forced to work out a compromise whereby the doctor would work with MassHealth on a case-by-case basis. This was the only route to ensuring the hospital and staff would be paid. Rikki had her initial consultation with the doctor and the doctor's team.

It was very frustrating to Rikki to remain in limbo after all this time. She was close enough to know her SRS *would* happen, but until it happened she could only dream of the notion of a full, physical transition. Sometimes she had to remind herself that her long ordeal would ultimately shorten the path for those who followed in her footsteps.

Rikki was in between bands and contemplating a move to a new town—one unlike Cape Cod with other towns bordering it. She had been on the Cape for a long time now, and she had had her ups and downs with the small entertainment community the Cape is able to support. As Rikki says, "Discrimination can be very subtle, but it can still have huge consequences."

Finally, finally, Rikki received her sex reassignment surgery. It was a big success, and she is feeling great and ready to move ahead.

Persia

Persia was about four when she figured out she'd been born in the wrong body. She can remember asking her mother what her girl name was, a question which her mother couldn't answer. In preschool, her mother was called in to discuss the fact that Persia wanted to play house, to be the "mother." When the kids got to dress up in the costumes the teachers amassed for them, Persia wanted to dress in dresses and heels. "Your son doesn't interact well with other males," the teachers said. "You might want to think about taking him to see some kind of therapist." Persia and her cousin Sateya, who was only a few months older, were often given baths together. Persia would ask why she didn't have the same parts Sateya had and when she might be getting them. Her mother tried to explain that she was a boy and wouldn't be getting any female parts, but Persia persisted in asking.

Persia's mother, who was only seventeen when Persia was born, had her hands full when Persia was small. She was trying to put herself through college, work, and raise her child. Persia's dad couldn't help because he was in jail. Persia and her mother lived with Persia's grandmother, who also worked. Persia was saved from feeling alone in the world by her cousin Sateya. They rode the bus together to their Catholic grade school, and after school they rode the bus back to Persia's grandmother's house. Since no adults were ever home, they went through their grandma's clothes and makeup and played dress up.

Since it was clear that Persia didn't want to play with trucks and cars or GI Joes, her mother bought her gender-neutral toys: teddy bears and electronics. Her first bike was purple, a more-or-less neutral color her mother knew she would like. Her mother also let her pick out gender-neutral clothes. But when she could get away with it, Persia stole the baby dolls she really wanted, often while shopping with her mother in the supermarket. When her mother found the dolls hidden in the house, she threw them out and gave Persia a lecture about her behavior, her focus more on the thievery than the nature of the merchandise taken. Luckily, there were dolls at Sateya's house, and Sateya didn't care if Persia played with them. In fact, all three of her cousins (Sateya had two brothers) accepted Persia unconditionally, just as she was, and when anyone in the neighborhood made fun of her, her cousins were right there to stick up for her, especially Sateya's older brother, who was very protective.

Persia visited her father in prison a couple of times a month. Like her mother, her father seemed to think Persia was on her way to becoming a gay male. Her father spent a lot of time reminding her that she was a boy and was expected to act like one. Caught up in Portuguese "machismo," he drilled this information into her, though once Persia and her mom left the prison no one really made a fuss about the issue.

After sixth grade, Persia switched from Catholic school to an urban-area public school. Because the Catholic school had offered a more stringent curriculum, Persia found herself ahead of the public school students; she was one of the smartest kids in the class. Being a "geek" allowed her to fly under the radar; no one bothered her much about the way she dressed or comported herself. When she began to sign up for dance troupes, it was simply assumed that she was a gay boy.

But when she became a senior, she began to present as female. She left home each day in gender-neutral clothing and changed into girl outfits in the bathroom. Her mother started getting phone calls again. The school had never had to deal with anything like this, and it became a huge issue. Persia's mom wasn't happy, but she wasn't really angry either. More than anything, she was shocked that Persia would make the decision to step so far outside the mainstream.

Just before she graduated, Persia's father was released from prison and returned home. The first thing he did upon learning that his "son" was presenting as a female was tell Persia she could no longer live in the house. The physical altercation they had before she actually left cut a hole in her heart. She had wanted for so long to have a relationship with him. For all these years she'd had to find ways to understand him, to love and respect him in spite of his crime, and now she wanted to be understood herself. She thought he owed her at least the effort. But he remained enraged. And her mother did not take her side. Her mother's position was that she'd had a choice to make; if she'd wanted to stay in the house and be part of the family, she would have done what was asked of her.

Things went downhill quickly. Persia moved in with a friend who was also a transgender girl. Persia had worked in retail through high school and always thought that she would go on to study fashion merchandising. But now that she was on her own, she had to make money, and no one in the retail industry was ready to hire her anyway. Persia was over six feet tall. She didn't pass the way she would have had to in order to land a normal job. All the transgender people she knew were working in the sex industry. She didn't have a lot of options.

Her roommate took her to Jacque's Cabaret, a popular burlesque and drag club in the Boston area. She met guys at the bar. She quickly learned that working in the sex industry was as much a lifestyle as a way to make money; her dreams of going to college to study fashion went out the window. She also learned that the African American transgender community working in sex was very competitive, very catty. The pool of men looking for relationships with trans women was small.

Many of the johns Persia got to know made their money selling drugs to upscale clients. In order to maintain such relationships, they had to find third parties who would go into the projects to buy drugs wholesale. Persia knew she was putting her freedom on the line by working with them, but she needed more than just enough money for food and a roof over her head. She needed money for breast augmentation, which in that time and place meant having silicone (or what she hoped was really silicone) pumped into her breasts in underground environments. She needed money for electrolysis and hormones, also purchased from underground sources (until she was nineteen and finally went to see an endocrinologist). Persia became a vampire; she had no life at all during the day. She was a slave to the men she met. There seemed to be no way out.

The older trans women who had taken Persia under their wing taught her that you had to travel from state to state, because being the "new girl in town" was lucrative, but it wore off when you weren't new anymore. Traveling could take you from making a couple hundred a day to making a grand or more. Persia traveled to New York, New Jersey, Pennsylvania, and beyond, mostly by train. She had a friend in New York, a scammer who would send her an Amtrak ticket confirmation number for wherever she needed to go. She never asked, but she figured he was using stolen credit cards to purchase the tickets, which he sold to Persia and other business associates for $150 apiece.

To make up for their disappointment in her, Persia presented her parents with lavish gifts, like $5,000 cruise-ship tickets. They never questioned where the gifts came from. Nor did they ever turn them down. Persia was busy traveling, so she only saw them infrequently, usually on holidays.

A lot of things can go wrong for a young transgender woman with no real role models. Persia had friends who were killed in the course of escorting. Others got hooked on drugs. Some got robbed. Persia lost several friends, a few to hardware-store-class silicone injections. A few others didn't die but had to have infected breasts or hips cut off of them. Because Persia was making good money, she planned to wait to have most of her procedures legally. But that's not to say she didn't personally encounter industry-related catastrophes.

For a while she was dating a big-time drug dealer—let's call him D. D didn't want her escorting other men; he wanted her to be his girlfriend. But as he was married, he required her to visit him regularly in the apartment where he kept his merchandise. He had a "friend" who would pick her up and drive her home in exchange for some drugs.

Other dealers in the neighborhood saw her coming and going and got to thinking that she must be buying "weight" and selling it locally for D, which meant cutting into their business in the area. They wanted D shut down. One night after she'd been with D, Persia went outside and got into the friend's waiting car. Their policy was that the friend would receive his payment for driving Persia home once they reached her apartment. But on this particular night, he wanted the drugs right away, before he started driving. They began to argue. Neither of them noticed the other dealers coming up the street until the car was surrounded and being sprayed with bullets.

The friend managed to pull away. Persia was unconscious by then; she'd been shot in the face and was covered with blood. But the friend knew where she kept his payment, and he pulled over a few blocks away and retrieved it (from her crotch) and began smoking it. Somehow Persia regained consciousness just long enough to open the car door and spill out onto the sidewalk and call 911.

Persia's surgery required work from the front of her face, including her cheeks and chin, to the uvula at the back of her throat.

Fifty-two titanium plates were needed to put everything back together. Luckily a plastic surgeon was in attendance along with traditional doctors and nurses. The plastic surgeon made sure her face received feminization procedures as well as the procedures required to get all parts of her face fully functional again. In some ways the tragedy was a blessing in disguise in that Persia received FFS without having to pay for it. But more than that, Persia realized that this was her "aha" moment; even though it would be a few years yet until she actually changed her life, this was the moment she promised herself she *would* change it.

Persia began looking around for job opportunities. She found a few, but either they weren't right for her and she quit, or she wasn't right for them and she got fired. Meanwhile her position in the sex industry was becoming more posh than ever. She was working with CEOs in IT, with professional football players, and with others. It didn't matter. She was tired of being the girlfriend no one wanted to take out in public; she was tired of all the promises that were never kept. From the very beginning she'd experienced a feeling of disgust whenever she finished having sex and received her payment. That hadn't changed. She stayed focused on getting out.

Persia was meeting a lot of younger trans girls by then. She had additional surgeries on her face and she was looking good; she lived in a beautiful apartment; she had a dog . . . she appeared to be living a great life, and the younger trans girls wanted to emulate her. But she realized that escorting was not the best thing she could teach them. She began to volunteer for a transgender organization. As the organization moved her along into salaried positions, she stopped escorting, stopped advertising, stopped seeing even the regular guys who would often give her money just because she was their friend. She transferred into another agency and took on a managerial position. She made lifestyle changes; she knew her decisions would have a positive effect on the younger friends who were watching her.

As of this writing, Persia works at Fenway Community House, a facility providing comprehensive health care, research, education, and advocacy for the LGBT community. She does workshops for people suffering from chronic diseases. She doesn't see her former man friends anymore, but sometimes she hears from them or about them. Some of them are incarcerated; others have turned their lives around as she has. Some went from making a quarter of a million a year to being homeless, because they couldn't get past their addictions. "You do it until you have money to get out or until it takes you over," Persia says.

Persia is engaged to a man by the name of Rafael, who she says is one of the greatest people she has ever met. He pushes her to achieve every positive goal she has. He watches out for her, to make sure no one takes advantage of her in any way. Although he works fifty to sixty hours a week, when she has to undergo a procedure he is at her side. When she is recovering from surgery—she underwent SRS surgery only a month ago—he takes care of her. But he doesn't force his own opinions on her. He loves her either way, with or without the surgeries.

Doctors Salama and Oates, at Boston Medical Center, performed Persia's SRS surgery. She is the fourth trans woman they have worked on and the first African American. Persia has nothing but good things to say about both their surgical mastery and their follow-up care. Thirty years after she first began asking her mom why she didn't have the same parts as her cousin, Persia finally has them.

FAQs

From Linda's Office

Laser hair removal is significantly faster than electrolysis as it treats multiple hair follicles at one time. The rub is that the laser is not for everyone. Laser hair removal works best on people with coarser, darker hair and lighter skin—which leaves out big segments of the population. Because the light energy from the laser is absorbed by the pigment melanin and then transformed into heat energy to disable the follicle, in people with darker skin color, and thus more melanin, the skin can compete with the hair follicle for the light energy, which can damage the skin. The darker the skin color, the more risk for burning, infection, and even skin discoloration. Also, the laser tends to work best on people between the ages of eighteen and thirty. The laser has an easier time finding the hair root for people in this age group for the simple reason that, like them, their hair roots are in their prime.

The second thing to know about the laser is that the FDA regards laser hair removal as effective method for "permanent hair reduction" when performed by a skilled practitioner. In less ambiguous terms, you can expect to have about 20 percent of your hair permanently removed from the region per treatment. This percent can vary with laser equipment and/or skilled technicians.

My Clients

Straight clients in my waiting room may sometimes encounter a transgender client sitting across from them wearing plastic wrap over numbing cream. It's not uncommon for the straight client to come into my procedure room whispering, "Linda, is that a man or a woman?" Of course that is never a question I will answer due to all my clients' privacy rights.

But I can answer when people ask, as they frequently do, what my transgender clients are like generally, how they're different from other people. I always say it's like having two people in one. If you tell them about a problem in your life, they can offer advice from both male and female perspectives. Other than that, they're just like anyone else.

When they ask me how it can happen that someone who presents as a man can feel like a woman (and vice versa), I tell them not to spend a lot of time trying to figure it out. Most of the transgender people I know don't know the answers either.

If a person who is biologically male decides the time has come to begin to live life as a woman, then technically that person has already transitioned. But for those who want to make more comprehensive transitions, the process can be long, tedious, and expensive. A full physical transition from male to female can run from $30,000 to $250,000, depending on individual choices. Many hours can be spent under anesthesia for FFS (facial feminization surgery), tracheal shave, body contouring, breast augmentation, gender confirming surgery, and so on. Transitioning individuals need hormone therapy with a physician and gender therapy with a psychologist or social worker. Also, many require speech therapy, sclerotherapy (a procedure to eliminate varicose or spider veins), hair replanting or restoration (or wigs), cosmetic enhancements, makeup technique instruction, new wardrobes, and of course hair removal via electrolysis and/or laser.

Because of these many expensive procedures, the transgender people I see generally have good jobs. They are doctors, lawyers, teachers, designers, scientists, contractors, writers, CEOs, CPAs, engineers, and pilots. They are smart; they are introspective; they are good listeners. But people at large don't know this. They are fearful when they encounter someone they suspect is transgender. Transgender women tend to stare at the straight women in my waiting room. The straight women think the transgender women are staring because they are having lewd thoughts about them. What they are really doing is imagining how great it would be to be them—to have that face, that body, those nice clothes, those feminine gestures, themselves. Staring at them is a compliment, and also a form of rehearsal for the day when their transition will be complete.

Despite the many changes that have been brought to light as the result of people like Caitlyn Jenner, former Navy Seal Kristin Beck, Chloe Prince, and Jazz Jennings coming out, transgender people are still considered "weird" (and perhaps worse than weird) in many social circles that do in fact accept gays. The rationalization is that gay people are men or women who prefer same-sex relationships. It's cut and clear. We all know what being gay entails. There are no maybes in the equation. But knowing that someone is a trans man or trans women tells you nothing about their sexual orientation. Who you go to bed with and who you identify as are two different issues. Trans people may be straight, lesbian, gay, bisexual, or asexual, just like nontransgender people. Once they've made their transitions, they may want to explore new relationship options that appear to be more in keeping with who they have become. Or they may be perfectly comfortable with the kinds of relationships they had before transitioning. And in those cases, there will always be the additional complication of whether their former partners will continue to be comfortable. Jennifer Finney Boylan, a professor, best-selling author, and political activist, is a case in point. She wanted to stay with her wife but was afraid her wife would leave her when she began her transition. Luckily, that didn't happen. She still lives with her wife and two sons.

Then again, many transitioning people need to live the part for a while before they determine the best way to satisfy their sexual needs, as well as their desire for companionship. Take Yvonne, for instance, who had been a guy with three kids and a job at the post office. She had a straight girlfriend, but eventually she started dating Dan, a Tai Chi expert who was a female but felt herself to be a guy. I removed Yvonne's beard because she didn't want hair. For her it was about how she wanted to feel. Yvonne and Dan live with the gender identities they are happy with, even though they are opposite to the ones they were born with. They've been together and happy for close to thirty years.

In some ways people transitioning are like teenagers. The world feels full of possibilities when you are a teen, and the future is full of unknowns. But we all know that adolescence can have its ups and downs too.

My hope is that as more and more transgender people come out, more and more straight people will be open to learning about their stories and accepting them. Generally speaking, they have gone through lots of trauma to get where they are already. They may have had to deal with the loss of family, friends, coworkers, jobs, houses, and pets in order to have the freedom to express themselves more authentically. Often trans women find themselves divorced because their wives don't want to be regarded as lesbians. Or their wives may stay with them but feel embarrassed and ashamed, and angry because lovemaking is no longer satisfying to them. Transgender individuals may feel very alone. Like a teenager uncertain of how he or she is being perceived by others, they may be afraid too. And all the while they are going through the losses that are the hallmarks of their decision to transition, they must handle the other traumas that we are all susceptible to—illnesses, financial disasters, etc.

Luckily we live in an age where support for transitioning people (and their loved ones) is available through both social media groups and forums and community groups. This has made it so much easier for younger people to come out. But there are plenty of people in their forties or fifties or sixties who had to live through the informationless "dark ages," when there was nowhere to go with their secret, when there were no Caitlyn Jenners or Kristin Becks to lift the torch and light the way. Today transgender people can talk to one another. They can learn who the best surgeons are. They can find out what therapists to go to in their community and which endocrinologists have the most experience in dealing with people like themselves.

There is definitely a shift going on. The world at large is making a small space for transgender people and cross-dressers—and many others whose lifestyles doesn't fit the reigning parameters—to thrive. In 2015 *People* magazine reviewed a book called *Becoming Nicole: The Transformation of an American Family*, the story of two identical biologically male twins, one of whom was certain he was meant to be female. He asked his parents when his penis would fall off, and when he came to understand that it wouldn't, he, with the support of his twin and parents, began taking puberty-blocking suppressants and ultimately had sex reassignment surgery just before college. In the same year ABC ran a special about Bianca and Nick Bowser, a transgender couple who are the parents of two young sons. Nick, who was born a biological female, met and fell in love with Bianca, born a biological male. They realized that they could actually start a family as they were, even though it would necessitate Nick carrying the children. They are counting on you, dear reader, to have become open minded enough by the time their oldest child is in grade school to accept them, because that will help to better ensure that their kids are *accepting*—when they learn that mommy has a penis and daddy gave birth to them—and *accepted* by others who learn of the anomaly.

From Linda's Office

Tammy spent close to $9,800 on laser work and another $600 for seven hours of electrolysis. She had twenty-two full-face laser treatments for face and neck. Thereafter she needed an additional eighteen treatments focusing on her lower lip, upper lip, and chin, for forty laser treatments all told. It was because her hair responded so well to laser that we only needed seven hours (420 minutes) of electrolysis to pick up the fine hairs that were left behind after the laser work. Part of the reason for this is because Tammy, who is only thirty years old, had very few gray or blonde hairs, which are generally finer and cannot be removed (permanently) by laser.

Tammy's total cost was about $10,400. Her treatments were spread out over a period of three years. Her decision to tackle her hair aggressively may be part of the reason her costs were what they were. Generally speaking, when you drag out the hair removal process, you give hairs in various stages of growth (including beneath the surface) a chance to come to the surface. You are likely to save money if you opt to undergo hair removal over a shorter period of time. Of course, other considerations have to be taken into account.

FAQ: What are trans women thinking when they look at you?

Yes, girls, trans women are interested in your vagina, but only because they want one just like it. You can imagine how difficult it is for someone who has known for years that "he" is really a she to look down and see that incongruous penis where a vagina should be. Once hormone therapy begins, the penis and testicles begin to shrink to about half their original size. For some people it may get down to the length of a thumb. They don't want to function as a male; in fact many during sex imagine they are performing as a female.

FAQ: Do your clients ever have erections in your office?

Trans women clients almost never have erections while they are in my office and I am working in their genital area. Not only are their penises smaller because of hormones, but they don't want to function as a man, so they don't. There are exceptions: in one case a client had to get off hormones for three weeks before SRS. I had to do a final check in the scrotal area. The client and I noticed a comeback: a semierection. We were both shocked and laughed, and the session ended. But generally it's not a problem; again, it's a case of transitioning being more about what happens between the ears than between the legs.

By contrast, I have worked on many straight males—who come in because they are cyclers or marathon runners or other types of athletes and can function better (and with more comfort) at their sport when they have less hair—who have had near erections. I can't reprimand them; it's not their fault. It could be the warm towel placed on their thigh that sets it off. The towel is there to cover over everything but the small work area. Luckily it doesn't happen very often, and when it does it is usually near the end of a session. The session ends immediately either way.

FAQ: At what age do most people transition?

It used to be the case that nearly all the people who came to see me were in their forties or fifties or sixties. They are still the majority, but lately I am seeing people in their twenties and even some in their teens. Some of these young people come in with their moms.

I have one client who started gender therapy at the age of seven. Her parents were guided by her choices. Now she is eighteen, and I am treating her, getting her ready for sex reassignment surgery. The doctors will want all the hair removed from her scrotum because the skin of the scrotum will be inverted and transformed into vaginal lips during the surgery. Because she started therapy early and was able to block male puberty, she does not have much hair to remove. This saves a lot of time and money, and of course it saves a lot of emotional and physical pain. Even the hair on her face is very insignificant. It is what is called vellus hair, otherwise known as peach fuzz. Most women will know what I am talking about, especially those with rosy skin. Vellus hairs do not respond well to laser removal and often need to be removed individually via electrolysis. (Only those who are really self-conscious generally want to remove vellus hair; most women leave it.) Some people elect to zap them with a laser every three months rather than undergo electrolysis. The zapping provides a temporary fix (thinning the hair out a little) for the problem, but the hair usually comes back, and, though it rarely happens, it *can* come back darker. This is called the "paradoxical effect." The laser may hit a patch where there is no hair; the skin thinks it's being invaded and begins to produce hair as protection! I've seen people shave, thread, or wax away vellus hairs as well.

Perhaps in time younger people will make up the majority of my clients. If that happens, it will be because society is finally providing the support people need to be themselves. But in the meantime, many people still tend to do everything they can to bury who they are, to find a way to fit into the life that's expected of them rather than claim the life they know they deserve. Consequently, many of them marry and have families, because they are always thinking, *If I can only follow the rules, these inclinations of mine will go away, and I'll be normal.*

But that's not the way it works. You can't bury who you are forever. So, later in life, after they've tried being married one or two or three times, after they've raised their kids (which is generally a joyful experience for them because they tend to be nurturing and compassionate by nature), they come to me as one of the first stops in their journey. "Take off my beard," they say. "Take off the hair on my neck. I want to see *myself* when I look in the mirror."

From Linda's Office

Jill, who first came in to my office when she was in her early fifties, visited seventy-five times over a period of two and a half years, for a total of ninety-one treatments. Forty-four of these treatments were for laser work, and the balance, forty-seven treatments, was for electrolysis. The laser work performed on face and neck cost her about $3,500; the electrolysis on her face and neck cost her about $4,000, for a total of $7,500 on face and neck alone. The reason she needed so much work is because her black hair was extra deep and coarse. She also requested one or two treatments on her legs, for a cost of about $400.

Jill's SRS prep required about thirteen hours of electrolysis, or one visit a week over a period of approximately three months. These 780 minutes of zapping cost her between $1,100 and $1,200.

Her total permanent hair removal (including her legs, which were only thinned out) was about $9,000.

FAQ: For those who do not transition, is there an age at which they finally can let go of the desire to do so?

In my experience, no. The desire to transition usually gets stronger the longer one puts it off. Family and kids can help to distract an individual, but once kids are gone and there no distractions, there is nothing left to offset the craving to be oneself. When Caitlyn Jenner was running, she was running from that craving. Remember, she came out when her children were grown.

I have one client who transitioned in her early seventies. Some people responded to her transition with the question, "Why bother?" This client, let us call her X, was married for over fifty years and raised three children. When her desire to transition got to be so great that she could no longer suppress it, she got divorced and started electrolysis and hormone therapy.

During the time I was working with X, she began seeing a psychotherapist, endocrinologist, and other doctors. Eventually she began living full time as a woman. She had her name legally changed (usually transgender individuals will keep their last name and change the first) and was then required to change her social security, driver's license, credit cards, birth certificate, passport, and so on. It's more challenging to make all these document changes now than it used to be because agencies have to be stricter in order to avoid instances of identity theft. (Birth certificate requirements vary from state to state. In some states you must first have SRS before submitting an application for a new birth certificate with name changes.)

After following all the protocols, X was ready for SRS. She was seventy-two at the time of the surgery.

Is she happy? Very. And while she met a woman she enjoyed spending time with, five years after her divorce her wife realized she missed her "husband" and wanted "him" back, no matter what he called "herself" now. But as X had found happiness in her new relationship, she had to reject her ex-wife's overtures, though she still sees her at parties and other events and she sees her kids too. The adult children are still trying to wrap their heads around the changes X has made, so when she knows she is going to see them, she goes for an androgynous look, tying her hair back in a ponytail and wearing a plaid shirt with jeans. They still call her "Dad," and she's fine with that. The important thing to her is that *she* knows she's no longer living a lie.

FAQ: Having watched so many people transition, can you make a general statement about how they feel afterward?

The journey to transition is generally a long one. My clients are so excited when the journey is complete. Most of them want to go out and shop, get manicures and pedicures, go to dinner, movies, theater, museums. Some want to go out dancing. (As of this writing, sixty-five-year-old Caitlyn Jenner has been observed at several clubs, dancing with friends, including Candis Cayne, the first transgender actress to play the part of a transgender character, in the ABC drama *Dirty Sexy Money*). They want to go to parties and parades. They want to go to bars and shoot pool. They want to be where the action is. Some travel with other LGBT friends, and others just want to blend into the crowd. They have hidden their true selves away for long enough, and they are ready to take their rightful place in the world. Some want to date right away, and others don't. (One client of mine stated she would wait for two years after transitioning and SRS before she began to date.)

Even if they are in their forties or fifties or older, they often feel (and appear) to be much younger after their transition. In a sense they are beginning puberty all over again, but this time it is the puberty they wanted in the first place; and while it is extremely gratifying, it can spark its own kind of identity crisis. Like a preteen or young adult, they must learn how to sit, talk, and walk like a woman—or like a man, as the case may be. They want respect and kindness, as we all do. They want to be able to say, "This is me, this is who I am." Give them a chance; you may be surprised.

FAQ: How long does it take to transition?

The transitioning process can take years—even sometimes a life-time—depending on the protocol the individual chooses to follow. I have seen clients jump through hoops so as to be able to transition within a year, and some of them do it very well. The rule of thumb is that a trans woman should live full-time as a woman for a year before she begins SRS if she is planning on having it.

One particular client of mine took about eight years to transition, because she wanted everyone to get used to all the changes gradually. Her method worked for her. She didn't lose any family or friends at all. Everyone understood what she was going through.

From Linda's Office

You will note there are inconsistencies regarding the amount of time clients spend with me. For instance, one person had all her hair removed over a period of only three months. Others have had their hair removal treatments stretched out over years. Such discrepancies have nothing to do with me; I don't tell my clients how often they should come in (though of course I make suggestions). The fact is that some people—either because they are afraid to have hairs plucked from their body, especially in the genital area, or simply because they wait until the eleventh hour to make their first appointment in preparation for their scheduled surgery—are forced to rush through the process when they finally begin. Other people want to extend their appointments over time because they don't want to shock loved ones with a seemingly sudden transition, or because of financial considerations.

Alasandra

Alasandra (Ali) was born in Los Angeles in 1956. She was one of five children, and she was called David back then. Her dad, a quality control engineer for a high-tech firm, was the kind of man who took pride in the array of technical gadgets he kept in his garage, the kind of man whose responses to questions were sometimes so well considered and analytical as to be puzzling for a small child. Alasandra idolized him. Her mom worked at an assortment of jobs over the years, from press operator to packer for a tool manufacturer to nursing home attendant to answering service operator.

Alasandra's parents were affectionate with each other, and even though they worked hard at full-time jobs, they shed their work personas quickly when they came home. Her parents were so devoted to the family unit and so conscious of their Methodist traditions that it would not be until Alasandra was an adult that she would learn that her older sister was actually a half sister. (At age twenty-two, her father had married her fifteen-year-old mother knowing she carried another man's child and ready to love her like his own.)

Easter week was a favorite time of year for this loving family. Annually, they would travel for miles from their home in Fullerton, California, to vacation on Lake Havasu, a large reservoir behind Parker Dam on the Colorado River on the border between California and Arizona. They celebrated Christmas in grand style too, filling the front room of their house with a tree that reached to the ceiling and garnishing it with homemade candies and gifts they'd created

45

for one another. Their holiday tradition included using colored glitter glues to decorate new ornaments with themes that summarized the highlights of each particular year. Over time these personalized decorations became treasures paying tribute to the past.

Alasandra spent summers with her grandparents, Harold and Ruth. Harold was the principal of a local elementary school, and Ruth was a first grade teacher. They lived in the same place where they'd brought up their four sons, in a hand-built home located on a property in Whittier, California, that included fifty-three orange trees, two avocado trees, and a wall of honeysuckle and boysenberry vines. Alasandra mowed the grass, fertilized the trees with mulch from a local mushroom farm, painted (more than once), and reroofed the house. Her favorite memories include time spent in the workshop where her grandfather would devote countless hours to making board games from scratch. Sometimes her grandmother would appear there, complaining she'd been hollering from the back porch and couldn't get anyone's attention. One weekend Alasandra took apart an old phone, removed the ringer, hung the wiring between the workshop and the house, and rigged up a doorbell button so that her grandparents could communicate. Years later, Ruth was still going on about how this simple invention radically improved her life.

Deciphering the Code

In spite of her rich family relationships, Alasandra's early school years were filled with moments of turmoil that were beyond her comprehension. For one thing, she found she enjoyed playing with her sisters and their friends more than she did with her brother (who was four years younger than her) or the boys in the neighborhood. When she was six, Alasandra asked her mother to dress her as a girl for Halloween. They used her sisters' things to accomplish this task, which was fun for both of them. Alasandra's neighbors didn't recognize her. They wanted to know where her costume was. They assumed she was a cousin or friend to one of the kids in the family.

Her sisters dressed her up in their clothes from time to time too, when their parents were still at work. Even after her mom got wind and decided it was not in Alasandra's best interest to continue, she and her sisters found opportunities to get away with it. When Alasandra was older, she realized she could "borrow" clothes from her best friend's sister without anyone being the wiser.

In school, Alasandra took traditional boys' classes such as woodshop, though she would have preferred home economics. She tried water polo because she hoped it would make her appear more boyish and more physical. She enjoyed being a member of the cross-country team because running gave her time to think. But she was the family pie maker on holidays.

In her struggle to fit in as a "typical young man" during her high school days, she joined a motorcycle occupations class. She and four other students had motorcycles that they were able to customize as part of their class assignment. The social life this group fashioned together included meeting after school and on weekends to smoke pot and take acid. Initiation into the group required visiting an oil donkey (the mechanism used to draw oil or other liquid out of a well) and, after drinking an entire bottle of hard liquor, jumping on its head while it was in the down position, hanging on as it traveled up, and jumping off at the top without getting hurt or killed. They also spent time hopping empty freight cars and traveling for a while before jumping out and catching a ride going back home.

Alasandra participated in these activities, but really she only wanted school to be over. To expedite the process, she took summer school classes, and by eleventh grade she had enough credits to graduate. But the school pushed her to do a bit more, so she took GED tests and scored high in all five categories. With her GED results and the extra credits she had accumulated, she was able to qualify for a diploma.

At age seventeen, she received enlistment papers from the same navy recruiter who had taken her to the location for the GED testing. That evening at the dinner table, after grace, her parents asked, as they always did, if anyone had anything new to share. When it was Alasandra's turn to speak she produced the recruitment papers and explained that going into the navy would keep her out of trouble. She could leave for boot camp in San Diego within thirty days if her parents agreed to sign the papers. From there she would go to specialist training in a facility in the Great Lakes region. There were lots of tears that evening, but also her mother and father signed.

The navy provided Alasandra with a safe place to sleep, food, and a chance to travel a bit while she thought about how her future might unfold. She had very few friends during her time onboard the light destroyer she was eventually assigned to, but she made grade as expected. On one excursion (called a "WestPac" because it was a tour of the west Pacific region), she lost her virginity. She was twenty and visiting an overseas cathouse. "Is that all there is to it?" she wondered afterward. She continued to go "out with the guys to find girls," but she felt lost much of the time.

At the end of her active duty as an E5 she received an honorable discharge. Thereafter she went to work in an auto parts store. She made more money in the next year than she had in four years in the navy. She roomed with another worker, cared for her car, and had a very limited social life.

When Alasandra's parents called one day to say her dad had lost his job and they were pulling up stakes, selling the house, and moving to Northern California, she realized there was no good reason for her not to move too. Moving day, she recalls, was reminiscent of a *Beverly Hillbillies* episode. It included a GMC truck (with a camper filled with animal feed bags) pulling a horse trailer containing a pig and a cow. Alasandra drove a Chevy Nova pulling a small Datsun pickup with a camper filled to the top with personal items. Her sister drove a thirty-foot U-Haul with the remainder of their combined personal possessions.

Their destination was the foothills of Lake Tahoe in Placerville, where Alasandra's father had accepted a job at the US Army depot. Alasandra took a seasonal job in the region building homes with an uncle who had a construction company. Over the summers she helped build nineteen custom cabins from the ground up. Over the winters, she filed for unemployment benefits and supplemented her income with whatever she could make shoveling snow off trailer rooftops at various local trailer parks.

After three years in construction, she found an ad in the newspaper for a draftsperson job with a small security company in Sacramento. Drafting was something she had picked up in high school and was good at. She got the job and started out doing simple layouts for parking lot control systems and wrought iron security gates for private residences. She and the computer programmer she worked with hit it off right away. They were both single and had common interests. He had a Triumph two-seater sports car, and one day after he'd had the oil changed it developed a hard knock deep within the engine. Alasandra worked out a deal with him; she would rebuild his engine if he would teach her to program. Thereafter, after work and during the weekends, she spent time learning to document and understand coding. It was the equivalent of learning a foreign language. It required breaking the code down into logical pieces and then rebuilding it. This procedure would help her later in life with personal problems, which, she realized, could also be broken down into manageable pieces.

In spite of the fact that she was able to purchase her own home by age twenty-four, her personal life was a mess. She was living with a "safe" person, a woman who had two children who were bounced back and forth between their parents. This was a casual encounter "with benefits," as Teri really only needed a place to stay. In her effort to succeed as a man, Alasandra also spent time with the widow who lived next door. Still making every attempt to fit the male model, she continued to tell herself that her occasional wearing of the women's clothes she kept in her closet was only a phase that would eventually pass.

After a time Teri moved out, and though Alasandra stopped seeing the neighbor too, she continued to believe she could succeed as a man. It was at a Halloween party at her place that she met her first wife, Betty. They became serious, and as Betty was not very keen on her closet full of women's clothing, Alasandra gave away or threw out everything, an act known as "purging."

Over the next fifteen years, Alasandra and Betty moved several times. They went from Las Vegas to Michigan to Sacramento to Saudi Arabia back to Las Vegas to San Diego to Gloucester, Massachusetts—with Alasandra always hoping to discover the thing that was missing in her life, though she could never put a finger on what exactly it might be. Drugs came onto the scene at one point. They tried cocaine, and the next thing they knew, forty-five days had gone by, their bank account was empty, and their lives were on the edge of ruination. They learned their lesson, and that trip at least was never repeated. But there were other problems. Betty, who had been diagnosed with bipolar disorder, required so much care from Alasandra that the four children they had by then were clearly being overlooked, and Alasandra's own needs had gone completely by the wayside. For the last ten years of their nineteen-year marriage, Alasandra acted as both mother and father to their kids, and the need to rescue them from such a difficult environment became the driving force for Alasandra and Betty's divorce. In the meantime, Ali moved into a small room in the basement of their house, living like a janitor. With this modicum of privacy she was able to start buying women's clothing again—or so she thought. Betty found the clothes and threatened to make Alasandra's inclinations public if Alasandra contested her terms for the divorce. Accordingly, Betty got the cash from the sale of the house. Alasandra got the bills, but also the kids, as Social Services had deemed Betty unfit to parent.

Alasandra didn't want to live her life alone without a partner, so she tried yet again to be the traditional male and created a Yahoo! Personals profile and thereby met Sue.

Sue was someone Alasandra could confide in, but only to a point, as there were issues she hadn't even resolved herself, and once again her women's clothes were packed up and tossed out, yet another purge. Regardless, Alasandra and Sue bonded in a profound way. They found comfort together, and a physical relationship that was more intense than any other Alasandra had experienced. Sue had three children, and with Alasandra's four, they had their hands full. But working together they succeeded in helping each of the kids to discover their own path through life.

In October of 2011, on the night of the day Alasandra turned fifty-five, she found herself alone with her annual bottle of birthday tequila. As she began to drink, she reflected on the events that had led up to the present moment. She looked deep inside herself, recalling incidents that had happened even when she was very young.

Alasandra turned on the computer and eventually found herself exploring a website that provided personal stories of people who were "transgender." She had never heard the word and wasn't sure exactly what it meant. As she read their stories, she began to see the parallels in her own life. After all these years, she experienced the feeling of coming home at last, of discovering that piece of herself that had for so long been just out of reach.

Thereafter, on nights when the house was still and quiet, Ali got out some of the clothes she'd begun to buy again and put them on. This produced a feeling of calm. Something had shifted in her thinking. She'd made the connection. After all these years she knew who she was—a transgender individual.

She had to know what was missing in her physical makeup too. More internet research over the following days and weeks brought her to information on hormones. She scoured websites for additional medical solutions. The more she read the more she wanted. Once breast forms had been purchased, she wanted and needed to have breasts, and a figure that would be enhanced by the clothing she most liked to wear.

In the meantime, she planned to talk to Sue. She owed her the truth, now that she had discovered it for herself. Still, Alasandra spent a week in abject fear before she got up the nerve to tell (and cry her way through) her story. At first Sue thought she was trying to say she'd met someone new and was going to leave her. In a way that's exactly what had happened; she'd met someone new, and it was her own true self.

Alasandra found an overseas pharmacy, and she began to take self-prescribed hormones, one to boost estrogen and one to suppress testosterone. By the end of sixty days, she knew for certain that she was on the right path. Her lifelong feeling that her mind was always racing had vanished; her moods were more even; she felt centered.

How Does a Two-Hundred-Pound, Bald Man Make the Change?

Alasandra started gender therapy in January of 2012. Three months of weekly sessions resulted in a formal diagnosis of gender dysphoria. Gender dysphoria describes people who experience significant discontent with the sex they were assigned at birth and/ or the gender roles associated with that sex. Another thirty days and a very complete blood workup found Alasandra in the office of endocrinologist Dr. Joshua Saffer, who is world renowned for his experience with transgender individuals.

By this time Alasandra was presenting as a woman on a daily basis. She now slept at night in clothes of her choice or with some Sue had chosen for her. Sue was still struggling to make sense of this sudden change. She had married a big, strong, hairy, manly man who now wanted to wear women's clothes and be more feminine, who was determined to put her maleness behind her completely in the future. It was not lightly that Alasandra risked the stability she'd found in her life with Sue for the peace of mind she imagined could be hers one day.

By April of 2012, Alasandra was no longer suppressing her feelings but sharing them daily with her wife. Her physical relationship with Sue had been robust at the onset, but over time it had begun to dwindle. During the first four months of her hormone therapy (after the three months without medical supervision—a bad idea, she realizes now—she began HRT, or hormone replacement therapy, under the care of Dr. Saffer), their physical relationship was renewed. Alasandra felt sexual excitement partly as a man and partly as a woman. Her breasts were growing and had become so sensitive that they alone could trigger a mental ecstasy that she had never come close to as a man.

Around this time Alasandra went to her first "open" support group meeting. It was held in old downtown Salem, Massachusetts, in a facility that was formerly the site of witch trials from the late 1600s. She was dressed as a woman, and driving there she felt that every person in every car was staring at her accusingly, as if she were a witch.

She went in feeling meek and timid and fearful, but after being warmly welcomed and listening to others tell their stories, she began to feel at ease. By the end of the evening she had traded contact information with the organization's president. A month later, at the next meeting, she was ready to tell her own story. The response was very positive, and afterward she told the president that she was interested in becoming a part of NETA. She had found a home away from home, a place where she could finally be herself.

By the end of the year, she had become the clerk of the board and the vice president of NETA. That same winter Alasandra participated in her first big transgender event, a symposium called "First Event" where over five hundred transgender individuals meet, attend workshops, and participate in interviews with voice coaches and with doctors—for FFS (facial feminization surgery), SRS (sex reassignment surgery), and much more.

Alasandra felt more alive by then than she had ever felt before. Her face and skin tone and texture had changed. Thanks to a "hair replacement" that adheres to the scalp, her hair went from a crew cut to shoulder-length locks. The way her mind was wired was changing too. She realized she was so much nicer to be around. But she was still only presenting as a woman part of the time, and that couldn't continue. She just could not see herself having two distinct lives to manage. She had to change not only her wardrobe but also her mannerisms, speech, word choices, etc. She had to learn to perfect her makeup, nails, and hairstyle. A teenage girl has several years to work out her feminine identity. She wouldn't have that luxury.

On bad days she would chide herself for having upended what had been a comfortable lifestyle. She dreamed about going away with Sue for a weekend, somewhere where she could be herself, where they could be two women who were lovers and the best of friends. But Sue's self-image would not allow his to happen. Alasandra remained committed to Sue, but she was more committed to herself. She couldn't help it. For the first time in her life, it was thrilling to imagine her future.

And So It Begins . . .

Alasandra worked in a high-tech environment for a company with a harassment policy that provided protections for individuals like her. They were very accommodating regarding her metamorphosis, but making the transition on the job still felt frightening and risky to her.

All the while Alasandra was growing into her female persona, she was participating in LGBT community projects and events. She found herself becoming a spokesperson for transgender individuals. She even contacted the mayor of her hometown and requested the pride flag be flown the entire month of June (which is LGBT Pride Month). She also contacted the senior staff at her place of employment about flying the pride flag at their main manufacturing plant in Gloucester. To her amazement, both requests were granted. On June 1, 2013, she was standing at the flagpole at noon outside of her place of work while a small crowd gathered with her to see the flag raised. Moreover, for the first time in the corporate history of this Fortune 500 company, they also raised the pride flag at their headquarters in Santa Clara, California.

As time passed, Alasandra became a nonevent at work. But at the start of the new year, she realized her time with Sue was coming to a close. Alasandra was just not comfortable having a relationship with another woman. She moved out of the bedroom they'd shared and settled in another room for the time being.

Three of her four children knew of her plans to advance her transition and supported her choices to the degree that they were able. Her youngest considered her a traitor, someone unwilling to be a stable force in her life. Likewise, Alasandra had the full support of three out of her four siblings. Her brother remained the holdout, refusing to recognize her as a woman in any way.

As for her stepchildren, they had never really accepted her in the first place, but once she began her transition, they denounced her.

She and Sue had guided all three of them through their respective troubled teens to satisfying adulthoods. But they dismissed all that and could only see Alasandra as a person who had "lied" to them and broken their mother's heart. There wasn't much Alasandra could do about it. She had to move on and be thankful for the support she did get.

Pizza Man: A Love Story

A mutual friend introduced Alasandra to a man online, and over time they developed a friendship. They didn't talk much about gender issues. Rather they shared intimate feelings about life generally and discussed their future goals. Alasandra was still trying to fit into herself, trying to accept her life wholly even as it was unfolding. She was apprehensive about this new and very personal connection.

Nevertheless, in April of 2013 Alasandra took a trip to visit her parents in Phoenix, and on the way home she stopped in Columbus, Ohio, to meet with her new friend, Lou, for the first time. She arrived after midnight and took a taxi to a nearby hotel, checked in, and fell asleep. She awoke the next morning to discover that one of her nails had popped off. Luckily, she was able to find a salon within walking distance, and they happened to have the exact color she needed. In the meantime, Lou called. He was still in New York, he said. His car had been stolen and his aunt and uncle were driving him back to Ohio. He would arrive in the late afternoon.

Back at the hotel, Alasandra decided to take a nap to try to catch up on the sleep she had lost in recent days of traveling. But she was awakened by a knock on the door just after noon. "What the hell? Who is it?" she called out. The response was, "Pizza Delivery."

She hadn't ordered a pizza. She jumped out of bed and threw the door open, ready to blast whoever had awakened her. But she recognized Lou immediately from a photo he'd sent, and she fell into his waiting arms.

Alasandra and Lou were soon living together and engaged to be married. Her job and location remain the same, but her new life evolves on a daily basis. A while ago her employer changed insurance carriers, upgrading to one with a policy that includes coverage for basic sex reassignment surgery. Alasandra's electrologist, Linda, completed the presurgery laser work necessary for SRS on June 30, 2014. Alasandra completed her breast augmentation in March of 2014 with a local plastic surgeon, Dr. Beverly Shafer, and in July she flew to California with Lou and completed her SRS with Dr. Marci Bowers. "When your dreams come true," she says, "you get to make new and better dreams."

Alasandra is also working toward a BS in human sciences, with the goal of taking the state test to become a licensed clinical social worker. Eventually she would like to do gender counseling. Her positions on the boards of NETA and ILCNSCA (Independent Living Center of the North Shore and Cape Ann) have provided her with the support to grow as an individual while also helping to clear the path for other transgender people. She is also the moderator of several social media groups, including Transgender in America and the Beauty Network among others devoted to the support and resources for transgender individuals, with over twenty-five hundred members in several of the groups. And she is a returning presenter at First Event, the premiere transgender symposium held every January in Massachusetts.

The town of Gloucester has flown the rainbow flag at city hall every year since Alasandra first flew it in 2013. Alasandra's employer has flown it both locally and at corporate headquarters. Lou and Ali will get married early next year.

Callista

Callista is Ali's daughter, though she, like Ali, was born male. Her knowledge that she was meant to be female came years before the day Ali announced her plans for her transition. In another situation, it might have brought Callista comfort to know she was not alone, but in fact, the news about her then-father derailed Callista. She couldn't help but wonder if her own transition would hurt as many people and cause as much conflict.

After years of drifting, emotionally as well as physically, Callista, who is now thirty-three, found a path. A trans friend and coworker (a guy) saw her struggle and gave her the support she needed to begin to deal with it. In 2016, Callista began laser treatments and, soon after, hormone therapy. In her attempt to reorder not only her gender but also her life, she began a regime of exercise and healthy eating—and a relationship with a man who "threw his hat in the ring" as soon as he learned she was looking for a partner. Moreover, she opened herself to new friendships and even got involved in a political group working to create bylaws to protect migrant workers. In short, once Callista yielded to her desire to transition, she grew into her truest self in every way possible.

Callista had her SRS in March of 2017. While we learned of her story too close to deadline to include it in full, we are happy for her many successes and grateful for the photos she has allowed us to include.

TJ

And So Goes Life

TJ, who is fifty-two as of this writing, knew pretty much all her life that she was meant to be a girl, but she never dreamed there was anything she could do about this grave biological error. Her family was a typical conservative family, very nice people, but they would not have understood if she had talked about her concerns regarding her gender identity issues. In fact, she believes they would have sent her away to be locked up in a mental institution. She had nine siblings, and they all behaved in a manner that was considered "normal," so she became the family weirdo.

Looking back on her childhood, TJ believes her mother had an inkling that something was amiss, but they never spoke about it. Since she had sisters, it was easy for her to dress up. She would dress in girl clothes with boy clothes on top. She even went out like that. Only once did she get caught by her mom. But her mom only said, "I'll let it go this time, but don't let it happen again." Of course it did happen again.

TJ made some effort to be more masculine in order to fit in as she got older, but her efforts were like riding a roller coaster. She hurtled from denial to acceptance to denial to acceptance again. Except for when she was in school (where she was a social outcast), she mostly stayed home. She didn't have any friends. She was a homebody. In her early twenties she did make a more definitive effort at masculinity: she got a motorcycle. But not even a month afterward, she had a bad skid and almost crashed, so she sold it.

She considered getting married, but every time she thought seriously about what it would entail, she realized that her "secret" was too big an issue in her life. It was always there, always in the front of her mind. She didn't feel like a guy, so how could she be a good husband?

And so went TJ's life . . . until about twenty years ago when she began to take hormones. She ordered them herself at first, through various connections, and was able to take them sporadically over the next four years. In spite of the fact that she took them irregularly, they helped; they provided some relief. She found a therapist too after a time and thus was able to get prescription hormones, but it was a low dosage, not enough to make much of a difference.

TJ had been living in Illinois, but she was forced to move back in with her parents in New Hampshire when the factory she was working at closed down. The move necessitated changing doctors, and the new physician was able to provide her with a better prescription for a higher dosage of hormones. TJ, who had always wanted to be a special education teacher, also returned to school. But in her final year, when she was very close to graduating with an education major and a special education minor, the dean of education sat her down and said the department had issues with the way she looked. At school she usually wore nice tops, maybe flats, but nothing overly feminine. In his attempt to remain politically correct, the dean never mentioned her gender identity inconsistencies. But he suggested that she switch majors, take classes in something other than education. "Go ahead and yell at me if you want," he added as he concluded their discussion.

TJ responded, "I'm not going to yell at you." She left. And she didn't go back.

Eventually TJ found a job as a caretaker for people with disabilities and moved out of her parents' house and into an apartment, which she still shares with her nephew.

TJ came out to her entire family via an email message about three years ago. It was the hardest thing she had ever done. All her siblings had married and had kids, and she had never been connected to any of them the way they are to one another. But they stopped talking to her altogether after that. Some of the younger family members, however, didn't see it as being as much of a problem.

Since then, TJ's mom has passed away. TJ still goes to the house regularly to help her father, who has serious heart issues. TJ has always tried to dress androgynously so as not to upset the applecart when she is around family. When she visits her father, she is especially careful about her clothing choices. Nevertheless, as soon as he sees her he shakes his head and walks away. If she pursues him, sometimes she can get him to talk to her about the weather or some other neutral subject. But other times he is only mean.

TJ has recently had an orchiectomy, a surgery to one's testicles. An orchiectomy ends (or significantly decreases) the body's production of testosterone. TJ's health insurance comes from a state program for low-income residents. She pleaded her case, and the program coordinator agreed that she was qualified to receive the funding for this surgery. Now she would like to move forward with additional surgeries, but the state insurance program is no longer providing funds for the kinds of operations she would like. So she is saving her money and biding her time. In the meantime, the orchiectomy has already provided comfort she didn't have before. TJ feels happier than ever. She wakes up happy. She was never very hairy to begin with, but now she is having hair removal procedures with Linda DeFruscio too.

TJ goes out a little more these days because she feels better about who she is. She's not 100 percent yet, but she is slowly but surely closing the gap between who she is and how she presents herself. TJ, who is about five foot nine and 135 pounds, passes in most scenarios. TJ has attended First Event, the premier conference for transgender people and their loved ones in Boston, and has made some new friends. One trans woman in particular has become a very dear friend. TJ is not nearly as introverted as she used to be. There are still challenges ahead, especially concerning family issues and financial issues, but other than that, life is good.

An Inspiration

Dr. Sheila Kirk

One of the wonderful transgender women who has had an impact upon me personally is Dr. Sheila Kirk. Dr. Sheila Kirk, who used to be Dr. Bob, came in to see Merissa one day when I was there, and I got to meet her too. She was married, a gynecologist with three kids. Over the course of her career (working as Bob then) she had delivered some eight thousand babies, including lots of twins and three sets of triplets. Sheila Kirk also wrote much-needed, informative books on hormones for transgender people.

In 1992 I was invited to speak at an industry conference in Washington, DC, and I brought Sheila, who had become my friend, along with me. Just hours before the conference, somehow I managed to get some makeup in my eye. Sheila took me right to the closest pharmacy, wrote out a prescription, and handed it to the pharmacist. The first name on her prescription pad was "Robert." Sheila was dressed as a woman and was wearing a long, blonde wig. The pharmacist looked at the prescription and then looked up over his glasses at Sheila, who was ready for him with her sweetest smile. He said, "Is this you?" I laughed so hard I almost knocked over a tampon display. There were several people in line behind us. Sheila said, "Yes, that's me." She was giggling too.

Later at the conference, when it was my turn to speak, I got up and talked about skin care and the different probes that can be used with an epilator (a tool of the trade) for hair removal. While I was talking, someone shouted, "We don't want to hear about skin care!" It was a huge audience. They had asked me to be there. They were paying me. Someone else yelled, "Let her speak. She's interesting. Let's hear what she has to say."

I went on for a bit, but the heckler had knocked the wind out of my sails, and I wasn't having fun up there anymore. So I took the liberty of introducing Dr. Sheila Kirk and inviting her to say a few words. She came up to the podium and immediately revealed that she was transgender. You could hear a pin drop in the room. She went on to talk about hormones for transgender individuals.

Sheila told the conference audience what it felt like to deliver a baby, how she got choked up every single time she got to hand a healthy infant over to its mother or father. She told the audience that her mom had a pair of red pumps, and when she was a kid, she adored them and wore them every chance she got. She had always related better to women than to men. She understood the way they thought. Her first wife asked her a few times if she was gay. She wasn't; that wasn't the problem.

Once for a Halloween party Sheila dressed as a woman in a floor-length gown and her wife dressed as a man, in a tux. That was a joyful experience for Sheila. She liked the way she looked. She liked the way the men at the party looked at her. It was exhilarating. She dressed as a woman for a costume party once again when she was with her second wife years later. Her second wife said, "Anyone who can put on makeup that well has been doing it for a long, long time." Her second wife had known about Sheila's inclinations before they married, but now she decided she couldn't live with them after all. She wanted Sheila to change. Sheila had already tried—her whole life in fact. She couldn't hide her true self anymore. She was who she was.

When she was in her midfifties and her kids had been to college and had ventured out on their own, Sheila put herself on hormones and began to talk, walk, and dress like the woman she knew herself to be full time. Sheila's story had a happy ending; she married for a third time, a woman who knew and adored her as Robert and adored her as Sheila even more.

The audience loved Sheila. They gave her a standing ovation. They'd probably never met anyone like her before. They'd probably previously thought anyone who was transgender was a freak, because, let's face it, that's how most people thought back then. In fact, it's how most people think today. But here was Sheila, as intelligent and articulate as anyone could want, telling them a true story about what it's *really* like to long for the simple pleasure of being oneself. They *got it* that day. Sheila opened not only their eyes but also their minds and their hearts.

Sheila donated thousands of dollars to the IFGE to help keep the organization going and to ensure transgender people would always benefit from the good work the IFGE does. As mentioned above, she is also the author of several books on hormones, which she wrote to enhance people's understanding of the subject. Dr. Sheila Kirk's latest book, written along with fellow authors, is called *Transgender and HIV: Risks, Prevention, and Care.*

From Linda's Office

Marilyn, who is sixty-six now, began working with us when she was sixty. She had a mix of hair, half dark and half white/gray. We decided to do laser first and then electrolysis. The laser killed off as many black hairs as possible, and we finished up the light hair with electrolysis. Marilyn had seven full-face laser treatments all told. She did fifteen additional perioral (upper lip, lower lip, and chin) treatments, once again because the perioral region has almost double the quantity as hair as rest of face.

She had eighteen laser treatments on her body (arms, chest, abdomen, and bikini line). Two treatments were for the backs of thighs, where she wanted the hair thinned out. (She didn't have much hair on the front of her legs and didn't require any work there.)

Marilyn's 99 electrolysis treatments and 31 laser treatments equal 130 treatments all told. On body laser she spent $2,100. She spent $8,000 for electrolysis. We then worked over a six-month period on her genital area for SRS prep. This took twenty sessions at $150 each for a total of $3,000, for an over-all total of $13,100 for hair removal on her face and body. She has completed all treatments and has had sex reassignment surgery.

Marilyn has been working with me for about five years. Most of her beard and facial hair was off in the first four years, work-ing about two hours per month. Marilyn didn't want to rush the treatments because of financial considerations; her budget was about $200 per month. Also, she felt a gradual transition would better enable her friends and loved ones to support her. Everything is coming together well for her.

You can cut back on time, pain, and money with the laser if you are a perfect candidate. Back in the 1990s, I had a client who came in five hours per week for fifty weeks, over which time we cleared 99 percent of her facial hair with electrolysis only. (The other 1 percent was soft fuzz that needed no atten-tion.) Back then it was about $50 per hour. So, for 250 hours of work, that client spent $12,500.

Joanna

It's More a Transition of the Spirit Than of the Body

Joanna knew in her twenties that she was meant to be a woman. But it was much earlier, when she was still in the single digits, that she first came to the realization that she was different in some way. She remembers cross-dressing at six or seven and hiding it from her family. Even then she understood that it would be construed as improper behavior, something for which she should feel ashamed. Any behavior that was at all effeminate would have been challenged by her "manly man" stepfather.

Joanna will never know for sure when the transgender feeling began. She thinks a tragedy that occurred when she was still developing in her mother's womb might have been the spark. Her mother was only seventeen when she got pregnant with Joanna. Just at the end of her first trimester, Joanna's father was struck by a drunk driver while walking home from her mother's house. Her mother suffered extreme distress at a critical point in Joanna's fetal development and still hasn't gotten over it even today.

When Joanna was three, her mother remarried. But it wasn't until she was eight that she learned that her mother's husband was her adoptive father, not her biological one. In a fit of anger following an argument her mother and stepfather had, Joanna's mother told her that her father didn't love her because he wasn't her real father. That Joanna was an Italian (and living in a world that was predominantly Irish) didn't help either. Her stepfather was not warm or emotional. He seldom even spoke to her.

In school Joanna got picked on, but she compensated for her perceived weaknesses by having a big mouth. Still, she felt that the other kids sensed she was different. In her effort to overcome her insecurities as she got older, she behaved recklessly. At age eleven, she started smoking pot and drinking. She rode dirt bikes, jumped out of trees, trained in karate, and eventually rode motorcycles. She became wildness personified so as to be able to fool anyone (including herself) who might suspect the truth, and also to release the energy built up from constant frustration. She spent a lot of time alone. Her mother was a "clothes hound." Besides the clothes in her closet, she had lots of clothes stored in the basement, which made it easy for Joanna to dress up. Joanna loved these opportunities. When she dressed, the self she became was closer to her real self than she ever got otherwise. But the cost of getting that close was that the rest of the time she felt totally alone and disconnected, and she suffered from self-loathing.

Joanna found herself on her own at age eighteen, and that was the best thing that ever happened to her. Out in the world, it was evident to her that in spite of her inclinations, she was actually a very solid person. She got a job working as a shipping manager for a printing company making decent money for those times. Later, she was recruited by another company to work in their mail house for an even higher salary. She felt good about herself, but she also realized she had hit a ceiling and wouldn't go much further without a degree. So she began college, studying business and operations management, and she switched to jobs in the music industry, working as a DJ and also doing nightclub promotions and running an open-mic jam.

Joanna had multiple job offers after college, but none interested her. Instead, she backpacked across the country with no idea where she might land. She had a girlfriend, Stephanie, who traveled with her. They stayed for a while in San Francisco, where Joanna took a job in the graphic arts. When her girlfriend got pregnant in 1992, they returned to Boston to start a family. Joanna tried to tell Stephanie about her cross-dressing tendencies, but Stephanie did not have a good reaction even to a small dose of information. Joanna told herself it didn't matter. They were in love. She would learn to control her desires and master her behavior, and everything would be alright.

Joanna felt herself to be a true part of this world for the first time when her first son was born. She became a very active parent. She read to him every night, and to her second son when he came along less than two years later. She coached her boys' sports teams. She loved parenting; her boys were all-important to her.

One day, Stephanie came home and found Joanna shaving her legs in the shower. It was time for Joanna to tell her that she was thinking of beginning to transition. She had been successful at compartmentalizing that part of herself for a long time, but now the pressure was too much. She was horrified to think of the consequences of being herself. Her kids were ages nine and seven then. She was in her early thirties.

Stephanie handled the information as well as anyone could. She did her best to understand. She began gathering information. She was good at talking to people and asking questions. When one of the Boston museums announced that it was doing a presentation on gender identity, it was Stephanie who insisted they go, although Joanna was terrified. Later she even accompanied Joanna to a Tiffany Club meeting.

Stephanie was alright with Joanna's secret as long as she was able to keep it hidden. But when Joanna decided to begin hormone therapy, everything exploded. Stephanie told Joanna she would have to find someplace else to live. Joanna turned to her mother, who told her brother, who told her father. They all had same response: you have responsibilities and commitments to the children. They weren't warm and fuzzy about it either. Joanna agreed, not because of what her parents said but because she could not leave her kids. So, she sucked it up, pushed it back into the closet. She still had a good life, she realized, a beautiful life. She loved raising her kids, and she and Stephanie had many good friends and enjoyed many rich experiences together. Yes, dealing with her own needs was a constant struggle, but she had a strong constitution. She practiced yoga to help deal with the stress. When she needed a different way of handling pressure, she got on her motorcycle and tried to outdistance it.

Stephanie suggested that Joanna begin to see a therapist, and she did. Stephanie also said she thought it would be OK if Joanna dressed occasionally as long as she did it when she and the kids were out of the house. In this way, Joanna was able to find some release from the ever-building pressure. But it was not a long-term solution. Joanna knew with certainty that she was a woman in all the ways that counted. She knew the day would come when she would have to make a choice. Would she keep swallowing it? Or would she simply become herself?

Joanna waited it out. She and Stephanie continued to live together, though it became more difficult with each passing year. When the time finally came, Joanna wrote her boys a letter, though she actually told them before she gave it to them. Her older son was in DC at the time attending college. Picking him up at the end of his sophomore year meant eight hours in the car together, lots of time to talk. As she had hoped, he had a beautiful reaction. "You've always been there for me," he said. He asked just a few questions. He wanted to know if Joanna was interested in men. At the time, she told him she wasn't—though he and his brother would later figure it out for themselves by listening to the pronouns she used when she talked about new friends and adventures.

Joanna told her younger son a few days after telling the older one. He told her he was proud of her and thanked her for waiting.

"I love you; I will always love you," he said. These words empowered Joanna. The time had come for her to be herself.

Joanna had been a school teacher at a charter school before her transition. By the time she was ready to begin transitioning, the school year was ending, she had her contract for the following year, and the laws regarding discrimination had changed in her favor. However, after the school learned about her plans, they proposed another agreement, which Joanna accepted. She did not return to the job.

Joanna went to Cape Cod to visit with members of her biological father's family. She had disconnected from them years back but now she reached out to a cousin. When her cousin learned what she was going through, she invited another cousin, a woman who had done research on being transgender for her master's degree, to meet with them. They hit it off right away. Joanna's cousin invited her to her home the next weekend, and the next one after that. Now Joanna lives there, out on the Cape.

Joanna had sex reassignment surgery in July 2013 at the age of forty-eight. Her appreciation for every day of her life has only deepened since. Her sons have informed her that, looking back, it was difficult for them when she first came out to them, but they'd stood by her then and always would. One of the things they wanted her to understand is how, to them, she changed into a whole new person that they had to get used to—while they and everyone else in *her* life remained basically the same. They have proven themselves to be amazing young men.

Joanna now works full time as development director for a nonprofit theater. She still does yoga regularly. She sees her sons and her friends and life is very good. Joanna thought she would basically be the same person. That turned out not to be the case. The change has been deep and beautiful. Once she was able to be herself completely, she was able to attend fully to her spiritual development. She says it feels incredibly wonderful just to be herself.

From Linda's Office

Joanna, who had dark hair and light skin, started hair removal at the age of forty-five. Her process took about two years, with forty visits all together for both electrolysis and laser. She had to drive one and a half hours each way to get to our office, so she was motivated to move through the process as quickly as possible. She came in twice a month at first and then tapered down to once a month.

Joanna spent $3,200 for thirty-five hours (2,100 minutes) of electrolysis on her face (including neck, chin, and upper and lower lip areas). This was subsequent to twenty hours of laser work on her face, for $2,800. In addition to these treatments, she required another fifteen treatments on her upper lip, lower lip, and chin, because her hair there was about three times denser than the hair on the rest of the face, which is frequently the case. (Remember, in addition to whatever hair is evident in any one particular moment on a man's beard, there's probably two or three times more hair already in the growth process beneath the skin.)

Joanna's hair removal all told cost her about $6,000.

Joanna's Letter to Her Sons:

April 8, 2012

Dear Shane and Austin,

Before I get into the reason for this letter, I have to tell you how proud I am of both of you. I love you incredibly, and my greatest hope is that you experience this depth of love for someone else in your own life. Beyond the fact that you are both physically beautiful young men; super intelligent; interesting; and of true, quality character (yes, I know you VERY well), my greatest joy and comfort is in the way you love each other. Austin, when you were texting Shane as I was telling you about Mom and me separating, and Shane, how you reached out to Austin when you broke up with your girlfriend, shows me that you count on and naturally rely on each other. That gives Mom and me an incredible sense of peace because, no matter what happens to us, we know you will always have each other.

Speaking of your mother, regardless of what happened to our relationship, I will always love and respect her. I married her because she is truly a good person. I also think she is the best mother you could ever have had. As you continue to read, please remember what I just wrote.

By the time you read this, I will have told you what this letter is about. I am a transsexual. In my own definition, that means that I feel an intense need to live my life as a woman. I simply cannot (and never have been able to) see my future self any other way. Each decade that passes in my life is an honest surprise because I felt there was no future for me. This feeling is so strong that I would rather be dead than give up the hope that I can truly live my life as the woman I am. That does not mean I am suicidal. Just the opposite: life is amazing. I deserve to be a part of it, and I still have a lot to do to realize my personal mission of experiencing what this beautiful world has to offer and sharing that with others.

Without having the words or any understanding of what was happening, I always knew. If you go back forty-plus years, I was aware that I was very different than anyone around me. There was no internet, television was limited in its content, and gender identity as a comprehensible topic didn't exist in my world. My parents, as you know, are very self-centered, and we never related at a personal level. They weren't aware of my difficulties, and I felt very unworthy and alone. As I got older, I still didn't have any vocabulary or frame of reference, but I went through a slow, lengthy period of self-discovery. I knew I wanted to be a girl, felt best when I was presenting as one, was terrified that someone would find out, and felt completely ashamed for being so different.

This caused years of self-loathing, pain, and isolation. I made choices that weren't in my best interest (like smoking a lot of pot rather than focusing on my studies). But I have been lucky. There is something inside me that puts up a fight. I moved out on my own, made my mark, and realized that I do have value and worth. When I was around twenty, I accepted myself as I was without really understanding my situation. I was able to compartmentalize and bury this aspect of myself and begin to grow in all other areas. When I fell in love with Mom, it was genuine. When we started a family, I finally, for the first time, felt honestly connected to this world. I had a place and a purpose. The two of you are the greatest thing that could have ever happened to me, and you are the reason I don't have one regret about anything in my life. Change one life event and you might not have been here, who you are, today.

I tried and tried to completely bury my gender-identity issue. That turned out to be impossible and simply not healthy. When you deny your feelings, no matter how logical, stoic, or tough you are, there are consequences. The repression of myself caused me to suffer at times. At other times, it affected my connection to the world. Imagine sitting on an airplane wing, looking down thirteen thousand feet and feeling nothing. The height didn't scare me, the lack of feeling did. I had to jump just to wake myself up. Riding my motorcycle faster and faster, taking sharper and sharper turns, just to keep myself tuned in. That is not peace.

Around ten years ago, I finally understood my condition fully. I even began the process of transitioning (that is, changing from living in the world as a man to being a woman full time). At that time, you were seven and nine, and, for lots of reasons, I came to believe that I had to make a choice between living as a woman and living with you. There was no contest. I again pushed this part of me down and stayed with you. Understand, this had nothing to do with how you would react. It would have been a challenge for you to deal with this situation then, but I distinctly saw it as something we could handle together. There was just no way I was not going to live with you. The magical memories I have of you are not big trips like Istanbul. The true magic happens in the spaces in between. The conversations at night after we read a story, being there when you were sick or upset, watching the small changes as you grew and developed. As I explained before, that is my greatest reason for living.

Also, you may question, was I being genuine with you all those years? Unequivocally, yes. I truly loved coaching your teams, watching baseball with you, discussing books and learning, playing games, and the million other things we experienced together. None of that was false. There is just more to me than you were aware of.

So, what does it mean when I say, "I have to live my life as a woman?" There are a few ways to look at it:

1. *How I feel like a woman (identity),*
2. *How I present to the world as a woman (expression), and*
3. *How the outside world relates to me as a woman (acceptance).*

Before I explain all that, let me provide a qualifier. I am speaking only for myself. Another member of the transgender community may have a very different experience or understanding of the situation than I do. Also, gender is not black and white. Masculine/feminine and male/female, regarding gender identity and expression, run on a continuum. For every example of "what a woman does," you will find a woman who does not and a man who does. Depending on a variety of circumstances (geographic location, generation, family, career, etc.), society may or may not reject that person.

Also, gender identity is a distinctly different topic than sexual orientation. There are straight, gay, lesbian, and bisexual transgender people just like there are straight, gay, lesbian, and bisexual nontransgender people.

Identity

What do I mean when I say I feel like a woman or see myself as a woman? I am finding this the hardest to put into words. When I close my eyes and think about this question, I see colors and feel essences. I want to be as concrete as I can and am resisting being poetic. Of course, much of this is based on my personal view of female and femininity. I want to speak of being more relaxed and grounded, but that is the result of allowing myself to be a woman, not what it means to be one.

To me, being a woman is being strong without being aggressive. It is about being connected to others without trying to conquer them. There is softness and a grace that is in me that has been repressed. As a male, I always feel that I am paddling upstream; as a female, I flow naturally. There is a universal connection between all living things and my fit in this is as a woman. I am very emotional and, as a woman, I am allowed to enjoy all aspects of that. Empathy and compassion are my driving forces. I feel it is more important to hear someone than to be heard (though I certainly don't want to be ignored). My feminine presentation is a manifestation of the abstract concept of female that I feel within. The response I get from the outside world is affirmation of the person I feel I am. We can talk about this more.

Expression

How do I present to the world as a woman? This is what you are probably most concerned about. There are a number of aspects to this—dress, physical appearance, mannerisms, voice, personal character, and activities.

1. *Dress—This (and sex) is what people who don't understand transsexualism think it's mostly about. Yes, I very much enjoy and appreciate female clothing, but it is not the driving factor in my decision to transition. If it was only about clothing, I would just dress up on occasion and be comfortable returning to presentation as a male afterward. People who do that are known as cross-dressers. I tried that, and it simply didn't work for me. I dress in clothing that I feel fits my personal style and is situation appropriate. For example, what I wear to a club on Friday night is not what I wear grocery shopping.*

2. *Physical Appearance—You have seen some changes already. I am growing my hair and having facial hair removed; I have pierced my ears, and, for the past ten months, I have been taking female hormones that are changing the shape of my body and softening my skin. This is incredibly important for me because, for the first time in my life, I finally walk past a mirror in the morning and see myself as the person that I am.*

These changes will also help me move more freely in the world. Women with moustaches get unwanted attention. I will continue to make physical changes so that my body matches my self-perception.

3. *Mannerisms—There are some ways of moving that are distinctly feminine. For me, this is not something I am trying to do but am simply letting happen. The Italian in me is physically expressive, so I have always had to watch myself carefully. As a young boy, I learned the hard way what is acceptable and not acceptable and consciously resisted moving in certain ways. If I may ever be accused of "acting" like a man, this is the area that is true. For example, certain hand movements when describing something, the way I move my head when talking or how I react to something I've heard. Now, I am simply not blocking what comes naturally. This is subtle and not overt or flamboyant.*

4. *Voice—This is something that will take effort for me to work on. A female voice has a tonal range that is higher than a male's, but there is an area of overlap. Just as in mannerisms, how I speak comes naturally and I am able to interact with the outside world with relative ease, but my tonal ability is limited. As a school teacher who talks all day, this is very important. Don't worry. It's not like I'm going from Barry White to Minnie Mouse. Maybe I'll finally learn how to sing in the process.*

5. *Personal Character—Other than seeming looser, more relaxed, or responding in a softer manner, I am still the same person you have always known. My values have not changed. What I did not approve of before, I do not approve of today. What I loved before, I still*

love. I still laugh at my own jokes, and still desire to help people and to try to see the beauty and truth in all things and fight for what I believe in.

6. *Activities—This really isn't going to change much either. I will still practice power yoga, ride my bike, read, stay up on current events, follow the Red Sox, continue my graduate studies, go out for fun, enjoy the company of good friends, and work hard to be the best teacher I can be.*

From Linda's Office

Billy Jean was in her late twenties when she began hair re-moval treatments. She had twenty visits to my office over a period of fourteen months. She started off with one visit per month for the first six months but then switched to visits twice a month for the next eight so as to finish her treatments before her scheduled SRS. We were not able to use the laser on her because her hair was too light. She underwent about eleven hours (660 minutes) of electrolysis, the cost about $1,200. The reason she stretched her eleven hours of work out over so much time was because her skin was extra sensitive and she found the treatments quite painful. There were times she could not endure it for more than fifteen minutes.

Acceptance

How will the outside world relate and react to me? This is the part that has caused me the most anxiety in my life. The fear of rejection is powerful. This question also has different areas to consider—general public, work, friends, family, and you.

1. *General Public—Believe it or not, I actually pass easily. "Pass" means to be out in public (say, the mall, a restaurant, movies, or anywhere other people who*

don't personally know me are) and be accepted as a woman. This is due to the physical changes I've made, the way I dress, and, more than anything, my attitude. One positive outcome from the situation where the government stole my good name is that, as painful as it was, I have the experience to reflect upon. It showed me firsthand that no matter what my reputation is to the people that know of me but don't really know me, I can handle it. For the most part, people are focused on their own lives and, even if they mock or knock someone else, they don't really care.

2. *Work—I used to fear losing my job, but now the law is on my side. That is, there are protections for people with gender identity and expression issues, and I cannot be fired because of them. I have always strived to be an outstanding educator and am proud of the work I do with children. Of course, my job is a very public one, and I will be exposing myself to considerable ridicule and challenges from people of wide-ranging worldly experience (or lack thereof) and personal belief systems. I'm ready for that. I look at it as a chance to help educate others. The colleagues that I have come out to (to "come out" means to reveal a part of myself I have hidden from them) have been extremely positive. I work with an incredibly diverse and extremely cool group of people. Exactly when I let the administration know of my plans is something I am still working on.*

3. *Friends—You know all of my long-term, good friends. I have come out to them and some of them have even gone out with me when I present as a woman. The response has been 100 percent positive. This speaks to the quality of the friends I have chosen and what it*

is that I base friendship on. These are people of true, positive character, and we know and care for each other at a level that goes deeper than gender expression. Of course, life is always changing, and I hope the people who love me today will love me tomorrow. As a woman, I have made friends with people who only know me in that role and it has also gone very well.

4. *Family—When I speak of family, beyond you, the person that has always meant the most to me is your mother. As you know, we have separated and will be eventually ending our marriage. As you also know, we have had other issues that have contributed to the end of our marital relationship. My gender identity issues have been a factor but, in my eyes, not the leading factor in this. While our relationship has changed, I will never bad-mouth her. As I said at the beginning of this letter, I fell in love with a good person, and I still love her. My desire is that we remain close friends and she finds true happiness and joy in life.*

5. *The rest of our family is aware of my situation. I say aware, but that does not mean they understand. Some people I told and some found out without input from me. I feared rejection and, for now, have received that from your grandfather and uncle. Hopefully this will change. Again, now that I have experienced it, I realize that it is not something to hold me back. Just like the sun, I rose the next day. Grandma Sylvia and Mom's family have expressed support, but it is my job to help them learn and understand just like I am trying to do with you.*

6. *You—You are what I care about more than anything in the world. When you were little, I did my best to*

expose you to a wide range of ways to look at the world, and I believe you are tolerant, compassionate young men. The only reason I did not come out to you previously was because I didn't see how that could help you if I wasn't going to present as a woman in front of you. Nothing, even my own personal identity, was more important than living with you and being a part of all aspects of your life.

Now, though, things are changing. You will not be living at home full time, and you are both independent young men that I know will succeed in anything you do. I still plan on being here for you, and you are still my number-one priority in life. Now I must make this change in my life, and I pray you will come to understand.

The worst thing, for both me and Mom, would be that somehow this news upsets you to such a degree that you internalize your suffering and fall off the paths of success you are currently blazing. You are both so strong and self-confident that I don't see that happening, but we must keep talking about it. The next-worse thing would be for you to become so angry that you shut me out of your life. My dream is that you use this as a learning experience, our relationship deepens, and you continue to rely and count on me to always be there for you.

I have no way to predict how you will react. Anger, sorrow, grief, surprise, or disbelief are all acceptable. However you feel is how you feel. Your feelings will most likely change over time no matter what. I ask that you allow me to keep talking with you and be a part of this process. Of course, your mother is always there too. You may be more comfortable talking with Shanti or Grandma Nancy and Papa John. That's OK and I encourage you to talk with them because they truly love you too. We have a relationship with a counselor who specializes in these issues and there are organizations for people in just your situation. Check out www.COLAGE.org. It will give you a document these kids of transgender parents put together. Anyone else you want to talk to, I respect your choice in that matter. I would suggest we talk about it so we can review any possible consequences for you.

As far as when you see me presenting as a woman, that will be entirely dependent on how you feel about it. I am not going to force anything upon you and will take as much time as necessary to work through your concerns and address your feelings.

Of all the people in the world, you are the ones I feared telling the most. To even think about causing you discomfort, never mind pain, is taking all of my courage and strength. I just have no choice anymore. This is truly a matter of life and death. I hope with all my heart you will come to accept and understand me and that our love for each other will prevail.

With all my heart and soul,

Dad

Jamie

Jamie is into *The Lord of the Rings*, *The Hunger Games*, *The Matrix*, and *Star Trek*. Now sixty-two, she has been watching and reading science fiction and fantasy all her life. One of her all-time favorites, *The Identity Matrix* by Jack L. Chalker, is a novel that begins when a backpacking college professor suddenly finds his consciousness transferred into the body of a thirteen-year-old Indian girl. The movies and books that Jamie loves best present worlds in which transformation is always possible, boundaries are mercurial, and magic is commonplace.

Jamie was born a boy and may eventually become a woman, but she identifies most with nonbinary transgender people, those who can move between genders fluidly. When she was three she had a fight with another boy and came in crying. Her father, a college professor who taught philosophy, told her to go back outside and "finish the job." She doesn't really remember the incident herself, but when others tell their versions of it, she recalls the reluctance she felt all her life to be involved in physical conflicts. Her brother was three years younger than her, and there were times when she was called upon to take care of people who had hurt him too. She understood that these episodes were her father's idea of learning socialization skills—and they were typical for the times—but she never got over the feeling that she was playing a part. She didn't like to hit or to be hit. "You could fight a little better," her father would say when he'd watched from the window, "but I admire your toughness." Her father had a serious alcohol problem that culminated in nasty fights between her parents, which only got progressively worse over the years. It wasn't until 1972, when her father lost his job, that he finally stopped drinking for good.

Jamie realized early on that she preferred the company of girls to boys, but she put her confusion over the issue on the back burner. In the sixties, there was nowhere to take a concern like that anyway. More important to her was that she do well in school. Her father had sailed through his entire life with straight As, and in order to have any value as a person, she felt she must prove she was that smart too. But she fell short; while she could get As easily enough in subjects she was interested in, unlike her father, when she had no interest in a subject, she didn't do as well.

The person Jamie felt closest to growing up was her grandmother, her father's mother. Jamie grew up in Boston, and her grandmother lived in Troy, New York, some three-plus hours away. Nevertheless, they visited often, especially for holidays. Jamie also felt close to her grandmother's two sisters. She did not feel particularly close to her mother, who was a high school teacher. "She was OK," Jamie says. "If my dad said the sky was red, she would say it was red too." Jamie called her on her complaisance over the years, but her mother would never agree it existed. "She liked to pretend she was an intellectual," Jamie says. The other person Jamie felt close to was her friend Richard, whom she had known from first grade onward. Richard had a *Leave It to Beaver* father (that is, Ward Cleaver, played by Eugene Hugh Beaumont), who represented the calm, pleasant, and easygoing father that she'd wished she had.

Jamie never had a girlfriend growing up. She got married at a young age, but it was brief and more about getting out of the house than anything else. In college, she got degrees in history and anthropology and considered going into law school or education. While taking a few years off to think it over, she realized she had expertise in databases and programming, and she found a job working with computer hardware in New York. "I got dressed in a suit and carried a case full of tools," she says. Eventually she went back to school and got her master's in software and database design. Later (in the early nineties) she joined the US Air Force Auxiliary (Civil Air Patrol), a volunteer organization that carries out search and rescue missions on behalf of the US Air Force and also serves the community in other ways. Jamie wanted to fly, and being in the civil air patrol gave her a chance to become adept. After obtaining a commercial pilot rating, she almost took a professional flight job with Crossair in Switzerland, but the pay cut would have been too great. (These days Jamie is working on her CFI, which is a flight instructor rating. She would like to teach flying. She is "current" and flies two to three times a month on average, with a total of about one thousand flight hours.)

While Jamie did not regard herself as a woman in these years, she continued to enjoy the company of women over men. At one of her early jobs, at a company called CompuGraphics, the men and women took their lunches in different locations each day, and one day Jamie couldn't stand it anymore and left the men's lunch group to dine with the women. She had become something of a master at the game of charades by then, but less acting was required when she was with females. It felt "normal," in fact.

Jamie met Yvonne while still working in computers, out in LA at the time. There was something about Yvonne's tomboyish looks and personality that Jamie liked right away. She wanted Yvonne— who was nineteen to Jamie's twenty-nine—in her life. They stayed together for a month in LA. They met in Paris when Jamie had to be there for a business trip. And Yvonne came out to Boston when Jamie was back home.

Jamie and Yvonne have now been married for thirty-two years and have seven children—four girls and three boys. The girls are, from oldest to youngest, a US Coast Guard officer, a registered nurse, a senior at the University of New Hampshire (and a member of the Air National Guard), and a second-year nursing student in college. The three boys are still in school.

Jamie's relationship with her family has always been good. She and Yvonne had much in common from the beginning. Like Jamie, Yvonne felt she had to get straight As growing up, in her case because she felt herself in competition with her older sister. Jamie and Yvonne are both hard workers; they worked at the same job together until their third daughter was born, at which time Yvonne became a teacher. They are both concerned parents. And they both share the same values. Jamie's mom is eighty-nine now and in assisted living. Jamie and Yvonne both take care of her.

But at this juncture in their lives they find they have a problem, and they have been going to joint therapy to work on it. About three years ago, Jamie began to analyze all those feelings she had put on the back burner ever since childhood. "Once you begin to unravel the ball," she explains, "you can't get it to stop. You wonder how did you go from here to there, and you look back on your life, and it starts to make sense."

Jamie began to ask herself what it meant that she liked females but also, if given a choice, would want to be one.

In recent times Jamie has gone for electrolysis to get rid of her beard—and it's a lot more comfortable for her without it. She finds that she can blend in at both ends of the spectrum now, as male or female, when she wants to. She has also worked with a voice coach and can now sound like a man or modify her pitch to sound like a woman. And she has had some FFS (facial feminization surgery), to soften her "guy" look. Frankly, she would be OK to leave it there, someplace in the middle, but society is *not* OK with that kind of equivocation. Society wants things black or white, A or B, one or the other. Jamie has elements of both male and female, but if she is going to be forced to choose, her inclination is to choose female. She's safer if she presents as a woman; she is less likely to encounter violence.

But this is all very difficult for Yvonne, who understandably worries about how other people perceive them as a family. On a recent vacation in Colorado, Jamie, who pushed herself to overcome her childhood shyness and is now very social ("People who have good coping skills can force themselves to do what they have to do," she says), started a conversation with a bus driver. The driver responded to her questions about the area with "yes, ma'am" and "no, ma'am." Yvonne was angry. They were traveling as a family. But as Jamie points out, families come in all shapes and sizes.

Jamie was born Edward, her grandfather's name, which she always disliked. People tended to call her Ed or Eddie, both of which she could tolerate. But as her need for gender ambiguity grew, she came to see Edward, or even Ed or Eddie, as a red flag. On the other hand, a name like Michelle was a red flag in a different way.

Last year Jamie changed her name legally. The idea for "Jamie" was embedded in the fact that James was her confirmation name; her parents, like many parents of that generation, had never given her a middle name. Jamie works well; 60 percent of the Jamies in the world are female, 40 percent male. It almost exactly mirrors how Jamie feels inside.

Most people call her by her name of choice now, though a few still call her Ed. She is trying to find a healthy balance in her life. Her hair is longer than it used to be, but not super long. She wears makeup, but not so much that anyone would really notice. She wears gender neutral clothes, as do so many people these days. She wants to be who she is without making anyone else feel uncomfortable. Full-out female attire would not work; it would feel drastic.

Knowing that SRS requires scheduling well in advance, Jamie has gone ahead and scheduled. She has plenty of time to change her mind if she wants to. But in some ways having the surgery is a safety net, especially when she has to travel to places like Turkey, where overt androgyny could easily become an issue. It can't hurt to have everything lined up, her body coinciding with the facial work she's already had and her excellent mastery over female vocalization. Once she's lined up, she can always go back into the middle when she wants to or when family relations require it. It seems simple to her, but when she tries to explain her thinking to others she can see they are often befuddled.

One place where Jamie feels fully supported is at the ELCA (Evangelical Lutheran Church of America) where Jamie is an assisting minister. The ELCA is a "welcoming" church; their mission statement is, "There is a place for you here. We are the church that shares a living, daring confidence in God's grace. Liberated by our faith, we embrace you as a whole person—questions, complexities and all. Join us as we do God's work in Christ's name for the life of the world." Jamie, who was always interested in divinity studies, participated in a two-year program in order to serve at ELCA. Yvonne and the children attend ELCA too. All but the two youngest have been confirmed there.

Will Yvonne be OK when all is said and done? It is Jamie's opinion that their bond is strong enough to make this work. She thinks she sees some lines beginning to shift. The other day she noticed that her button-down shirt and Yvonne's button-down were both hanging on the back of the door, and they didn't really look any different. She took a picture of them and sent it to Yvonne with a note: "Whose is whose?"

FAQs

From Linda's Office

In order to be certain you are done with facial hair removal, you must go at least six months with no new growth. Still, there is always the possibility of rogue hair growth resulting from trauma on some area of the skin, changes in hormones, medication, and/or just because your facial skin is living matter like the rest of you and hence is always in a state of flux. Rogue hairs may require touch ups once a year or so, depending on circumstances. If you see a rogue hair between touch-up appointments, don't tweeze, pluck, thread, wax, or sugar it, and don't use any depilatory creams on it. Simply snip it or lightly shave it.

FAQ: Does electrolysis take a long time?

Clients come to me early on, sometimes even before they've begun hormone therapy. In some cases we will spend hundreds of hours together over a period of months or even years.

Electrolysis (like the other transition components) works best when sessions are spread out over time, and most clients prefer it that way because they want their change to be gradual so that the people in their lives may pick up that something is different *gradually* and therefore be less shocked—and more accepting—when the announcement is finally made.

There are a few locations where an individual can have anesthesia and sit for hours to have electrolysis within a few very long sessions. The trauma to the face is greater than the slower process.

FAQ: Do straight men undergo facial hair removal too?

Yes! These days many men opt to have a more professional appearance. Having the hair removed from their necks, front and back, can ensure they look their best when they are dressed in suits. Removing hair from brows (or breaking up a unibrow), nostrils, the outer nose, and ears can also give them a cleaner appearance. Some guys have the hair removed from their chests, shoulders, upper arms, and backs too, so that they don't look so hairy at the beach.

FAQ: How does an electrologist prepare a client for sex reassignment surgery?

During the prep for SRS, electrologists and laser hair technicians remove hair from the male scrotum and bikini area. A lot of my straight clients are college-age women who want Brazilians because it makes them feel cleaner, fresher, and less worried about stray pubic hairs materializing from under their panties or bikini bottoms. Many trans women want the same thing—for the same reasons.

Brazilian hair removal can mean full removal of all hair in the area or partial. Some women and trans women want Brazilians that leave behind only a strip of hair—called a landing strip—or that leave behind only a neat triangle. Others want custom designs. The SRS doctors like a little hair to cover the scarring area near the neovagina, although in time the scars fade.

Although most doctors in the United States prefer electrolysis, there are doctors who prefer scraping of the hair follicles on the genitals themselves, as opposed to electrolysis (or possibly laser), in preparation for SRS.

FAQ: Can transgender people get laser hair removal covered under health insurance?

More and more companies are coming on board to cover SRS permanent hair removal prep. I have seen insurance companies pay for the face and body. If an insurance company rejects a transgender individual's claim, they can resubmit for an appeal.

Chrissy
A Year of Living Precariously

Chrissy, previously Edward, is fifty-nine at the time of this writing. She only recently made her transition from male to female in the physical sense of the word in a hospital in Phoenix. Of course her real transition started long ago.

When people ask Chrissy how she came to be a woman in a man's body, she suggests the answer may lie in her medical history. She could be one of the many people who was effected by medications their mothers took while pregnant, resulting in children born with the bodies of boys but with female brains. The medication in question may have been DES (diethylstilbestrol), a synthetic form of estrogen heavily prescribed by doctors from 1938 until 1971 to help prevent miscarriages. Many researchers believe that man-made estrogen passed down in this way to male embryos could have resulted in gender dysphoria. Or the normal sequence of embryonic development may simply not have unfolded properly. Either way, if you discover when you are very young that while you look like a boy, you think like a girl, what can you do about it?

There were seven kids in Chrissy's family, six of them boys. Chrissy had dump trucks just like her brothers. She was athletic and physically fit. But she would look at her sisters and female cousins and wonder why she couldn't be like them, act like them, play their games, wear their dresses. Chrissy was a member of an Irish Catholic family. She grew up in the '50s and '60s, when boys played boys' games with other boys and girls played girls' games with other girls. There was no crossover, except maybe occasionally for games like hide-and-go-seek. She had nowhere to go with her questions. If she had told someone in her community that she wanted to wear dresses, they may have sent her off for electric shock treatments, which was not an uncommon remedy back then.

Chrissy did exceptionally well at being a boy—though given her family and the norms of her community, she had lots of incentive. However, she truly loved baseball and became a champion at batting. In 1967 she had a higher batting average than Ted Williams. But in other areas of her "boyhood," she knew she was only faking it, and when she was about twelve she started making trips to the bookstore to see if she could find information that would help her sort things out. There wasn't much available back in those days, and since she couldn't very well ask a clerk for help, she left without any answers. Her dilemma was this: there was a dialogue going on in her head constantly, between Edward and the female she more easily identified with. She had to give her a name, so she began to call herself Christine.

Edward and Christine argued all the time. Eddie just wanted to play sports and be left alone. He didn't want Christine in there bugging him. Eddie was tall and thin and wiry. He wasn't the fastest, but he could get out of the way when he had to. As he got older, he played soccer, hockey, and track and skied. He preferred to play gently, but he was always ready to go in the other direction. Once while playing hockey, he nailed a guy so bad on the boards that he flipped head over heels, and Eddie stole the puck just as the whistle blew. He'd given the guy an education, he felt. After that, the guy passed the puck when he was near. Eddie could handle himself. He was a bit underdeveloped; he didn't look strong. But he was strong.

Christine, however, could beat the hell out of Eddie emotionally, and they both knew it. Eddie tried to ignore her and resume his focus on sports. He was determined to show himself as a gifted athlete. But no matter how hard he played, no matter how high his achievements piled up, Christine refused to leave.

Family life was good as long as Chrissy kept up the pretense of being who her family thought she was. Summers were spent in mountains or at the beach, fishing, swimming, playing tennis, horseback riding, biking, sailing, and so on. Back home she became interested in "muscle" cars, corvettes, roadsters, and a '66 GTO she rebuilt. Typical macho behavior; no one would have guessed her secret.

As Chrissy got older she came to believe that she had a split personality. But what she read about dissociative identity disorder didn't quite jibe, because, unlike others suffering from DID, she didn't feel like Eddie some of the time and Christine at other times. She felt like both of them all the time. In fact, if there was a pull in one direction more than the other, it favored Christine. She was Christine being forced to live Eddie's life. It was difficult to form close relationships under those circumstances. She had acquaintances but very few friends.

After graduating from her all-boys, Jesuit-run Catholic high school (where she was molested by a Jesuit priest as a teenager), Chrissy attended Northeastern University and majored in accounting. Everyone on the college hockey team spoke French and she didn't, so she didn't make the team. She tried for the ski team instead. She got on and got good and started racing. She even won a few races. She also learned to fly planes. Her parents owned a resort, and in the summers she worked there, doing maintenance side by side with her father. She also worked as a chef.

Chrissy dated only four women in her life, and she married two of them. She met her first wife, Julie, in a hospital, where Julie, a nursing student, was working and Chrissy was recovering from a ski accident. Julie came on to her, and Chrissy's testosterone responded. When she masturbated or had sex, Chrissy would flip the roles around. She would imagine *she* was the woman and *her partner* was the one performing the penetration; it was very confusing and troublesome.

Their relationship was up and down. Chrissy suffered from "raging immaturity." But Julie wanted to have sex and professed to love Chrissy, and Chrissy wanted to have sex too, so they got married. Chrissy believed that being married would help her slough off her lifelong feeling that she was really a woman on the inside. But in fact, that's not what happened. She continued to imagine herself as a woman when she and Julie had sex. Sometimes she disappeared, getting a room in a hotel where she could wear women's clothes or, if she didn't have any with her, then wrap sheets around herself. She needed that outlet.

After college Chrissy got a job in New York, working for a Fortune 500 company, but she hated it. Then she learned about two guys she knew back in Boston who had a nightclub and needed a third guy to help with finances. Having majored in accounting and having been involved with money management at her parents' hotel, she had the requisite training and understanding of how hospitality businesses should be run from a fiscal perspective.

The club, called Uncle Sam's, was located on Nantasket Beach, Massachusetts. Six months into her work there, Chrissy started doing coke. Others were doing it too. It was a common thing to do. They were all making good money. It was the '80s, and drugs were everywhere. Her life was like a nonstop night at Studio 54. Everyone came into to Uncle Sam's. Though she hadn't had her own motorcycle since college, she hung out with bikers, Hells Angels and the Red Emeralds. On the music end, she got to meet the Ramones, Rick Derringer, Steven Stills, Johnny Winter, Leon Russell, Cheap Trick, Joe Cocker, and on and on. But while "Eddie" appeared to be as dynamic a guy as ever, Christine was never out of the picture, not for a minute. Chrissy continued to dress in secret as often as possible. She had so much to lose if she got caught, but it was a risk she had no choice but to take.

One night Chrissy and a partner found themselves with tickets to see the Rolling Stones on their opening night in Philadelphia. They rounded up several friends, and they all got into a minivan and drove down to Philly. The problem was that they had left directly from Uncle Sam's in the wee hours of the morning, and Chrissy had not had a chance to deposit the previous night's receipts, about $15,000 worth. She was carrying the money in a brown paper bag. One of her fellow travelers suggested they cut out a seat cushion and hide the stash there. Another thought Chrissy was better off keeping it in the bag and carrying it with her, wherever they went. Chrissy decided to wire it to the club's account before the concert got started.

They located a bank, and Chrissy went in and told the woman at the counter that she wanted to make a wire transfer. The woman asked how much. When Chrissy told her the approximate amount, she said she would have to fill out forms for the IRS. It was clear the woman suspected they were drug dealers. Chrissy told her to go ahead and get the forms. Then Chrissy and her friend went into a private room in the back so they could count the bills and get an exact amount. They counted. They did coke too. They counted some more and did more coke.

An hour later they were done. Somehow they managed to get the transfer completed. They got the receipt, went to the concert, had a fabulous time, and drove home. But Chrissy knew her days of nonstop drugs were numbered. Something had to change. The trip had been good, and she had enjoyed herself, but there were days on end when all she wanted was to be alone so she could let Christine exist for a while. She was ashamed. She hated herself. She was a transvestite, or so she thought at the time. Transvestites were disgusting. Everything she'd learned in the Catholic Church suggested she should hate herself. She didn't want any part of being a transvestite. She remained terrified of being found out. She was able to live life recklessly only because she didn't care if she lived or died. In fact, she expected to die. Her family believed in control; if you wanted to, you could control anything. But the presence of Christine was something Chrissy could not restrain or control.

Altogether Chrissy was two years at Uncle Sam's. After leaving she started her own accounting business and tried for a more balanced lifestyle. She divorced and remarried. She had had one child with Julie, and now she had a second one with Gloria. She had savings from her club days. On the outside everything was just as good as it gets. On the inside the pressure was mounting. Eventually Chrissy had to face the fact that she couldn't go on the way she was anymore.

When Chrissy's desire to kill herself became absolutely unbearable, she came up with a compromise: she would come out—she would force herself to do it—and if it backfired and she didn't feel any happier after a year, she would go ahead with plan A and put an end to it. This was not an easy decision to make. If she had been thinking only of her family, she would have simply killed herself then and there, because her suicide would be more easily accepted than her truth. It would save the family a lot of embarrassment. But for once she was thinking of herself. She was giving herself a gift, a year to see if there was any chance that she could experience happiness, as a woman, as Christine.

And so it began. Given her own feelings about "transvestites," coming out was beyond difficult. It was nearly impossible. But she did it properly, with the help of a therapist and an endocrinologist who put her on hormone therapy. Since Chrissy is six feet tall, she was already taller than most women, but she learned right away that being a woman is more about presence and attitude than about height. Finally she could wear what she wanted to. She began to feel better. She began to feel some relief. The first year passed, and she did not kill herself, and her health and self-respect greatly improved.

But the reaction of those around her was as disturbing as she had surmised it would be. Chrissy's wife, Gloria, was furious. She was determined that her mission in life would be to ensure her child took her side against her father. A judge sided with Gloria by concluding that Chrissy's claims of transgender abuse were insubstantial. Nor would the judge recognize the instances of child abuse, bullying, and parental alienation that were going on. Chrissy was heartbroken. It was hard for Chrissy to reconcile how good she was beginning to feel with how upset everyone around her was. Her family, including her five siblings, disowned her. (One brother had died of cancer at the beginning of Chrissy's transition.) One of her brothers even joined forces with Gloria in a court battle to try to prevent Chrissy from seeing her younger daughter. Only a niece and a nephew offered any support.

It took four years from the time Chrissy came out to the day of her sex reassignment surgery. While she has been abandoned by many of her loved ones—her own father, ninety at the time, punched her in the chest the week before her surgery and would have taken a second shot if Chrissy had not grabbed his wrist— Christine continued to see her father, though it was very difficult for her to experience his physical and emotional abuse and bullying. Nevertheless, since her transition she has made many new friends.

Before she went into the hospital to conclude her transition, Chrissy sent out letters to her clients so that they would know what to expect when she returned to work. Nothing is easy. Her senior accountant quit. Chrissy had to hire someone quickly to hold down the fort while she was in the hospital and through her recovery, which would take about a month. She hired another guy, but it was clear that wasn't going to work out. In the meantime, her recep-tionist, who was pregnant, had her twins prematurely and had to leave too. Then there was a problem with the software the company used, and Chrissy wasn't able to print client returns. A tech support person had to come for days in succession.

Chrissy's surgery had been scheduled two years in advance. She didn't have the option of putting it off until her office got back in balance. So she went, but she returned to a vast number of angry emails, calls from clients wanting to know why their returns weren't getting done and where everyone was, etc. The only good thing, or so she thought at the time, was that Paula had managed to get back to work during Chrissy's recovery. But even that show of loyalty had a counterpart. Paula's fiancé hung himself in the days before Chrissy returned to the office, and Paula had to leave once again.

Did Chrissy lose business? Yes. Some people, ignorant of the fact that her senior accountant—her right hand man—quit for family reasons, made the assumption that his departure had something to do with Chrissy's transition—which it did not. Chrissy was disinvited to her father's ninetieth birthday party. A few weeks after the event her ex-wife suggested Chrissy kill herself and make life easier for everyone.

But on the other end, Chrissy knew she'd batted a home run with her transition early on when she was still in the hospital. And in spite of all the office confusion, plenty of people turned out to be fine with the information. (Her senior accountant did, in fact, return to the office.) Female friends who once thought Chrissy was trying to hit on them began to confide in her, sharing secrets that they had never spoken of before. Chrissy found she had become a better listener, eager to understand, and could help others. To that purpose she joined the board of a large, nonprofit, Boston-based LGBT youth organization.

Amazingly to her, Chrissy is discovering that she is actually a fairly well-adjusted person. She is a drug-free, high-functioning lover of life. "Eddie" is still there in some sense, but he and Christine have bonded. Now she can laugh about the some of the struggles they endured together. She says being a sports-loving guy was a cool disguise that got her into lots of locker rooms.

She may have spied on men for years, but she knows this: she never was one.

About a year and a half ago, Chrissy submitted a multipage document and motion to the court which documented evidence of her abuse by her ex-wife and the shunning and isolation of her two daughters with her.

Chrissy felt the outcome of the case was unfair and that the judge didn't follow protocol when he assigned child support higher than her gross income. She felt the judge didn't take into account any of the documentation she had sent, her trauma, or the circumstances she faced. She wasn't found guilty of anything.

Her therapist deemed her unstable and caused her to be arrested for an alleged threat to the judge. She spent ten days in the hospital and fifty days in prison, where she was confined from ten to fifteen hours a day. She lost about two-thirds of her clientele of her business. With this new trauma, she is back on antidepressants, mood stabilizers, and anxiety prescriptions. A restraining order is in place, and Chrissy's ex has coached the children not to visit or see her, further dividing her from her family.

In spite of all these challenges, she recently published her first children's book, called *My First Red Sox Game*.

From Linda's Office

We began Chrissy's sessions with laser on her face, neck and beard, legs, and SRS area so that we could reduce electrolysis hours as much as possible. As mentioned previously in these pages, laser only works on darker hairs, while electrolysis is necessary for lighter hairs. The cost for Chrissy's laser work was about $3,500.

Chrissy began electrolysis in her midfifties. With regular visits, most of her hair was gone after two years. The following two years were spent with what I call nuisance hairs, finer hairs that most trans women like to have completely cleaned up so their skin is smooth. We spent about 2,400 minutes (forty hours) on her electrolysis (meaning under the probe or needle), at a cost of about $3,800—1,800 minutes (thirty hours) on her face and neck and 600 minutes (ten hours) prepping for SRS.

The total spent for Chrissy's hair removal was about $7,300. She had twenty-five sessions for laser work and fifty for electrolysis. Some of her office visits included work with both laser and electrolysis.

By comparison, Sue, a biological woman in her early thirties with lots of vellus (soft, thin, downy) facial hair also came in for about two years, or 2,400 minutes (forty hours) over fifty sessions just like Chrissy. They spent approximately the same amount of money too.

Sam

Sam, who is fifty as of this writing, came out three years ago. Since then he has inspired many people with his courage, and in turn many people have inspired him with their kind responses to his journey.

Sam suspected from a very young age that he was different, but back in the sixties and seventies there were no words to express what he was feeling. Girls who felt masculine were called tomboys, and that was the closest he could come in identifying himself.

Sam grew up with three brothers. Wearing his older brother's hand-me-downs and playing with all his brothers' toys was acceptable in a home dominated by male presence. His parents were kindhearted and tried to understand his needs. They preferred their "daughter" to wear dresses, but they acknowledged Sam's inclinations too. They even allowed Sam to have his hair cut very short like his brothers.

Even with the short hair and the tomboy clothing, though, Sam couldn't get where he needed to be. There was no therapy available at that time for people in his situation. No one even thought about changing their gender. The notion was the equivalent, Sam says, of deciding to become a superhero. No one can fly; it's just not possible. So he sucked it up; he conformed.

He tried to be a girl as much as was necessary. He tried to like boys. But whenever one wanted to get more intimate with him, he found himself running for the hills. As he got older he began to know girls who identified as lesbians, and he thought maybe that would get him closer to who he really was. "Everyone is trying to fit in, to find a place or group of people and community that they can better identify with," he explains. He didn't really identify completely, but it seemed a step in the right direction. And many of the lesbians he knew were tomboys too.

Twenty years ago, Sam fell in love with Lisa, and, as same-sex marriage was still a pipe dream, they had a commitment ceremony. They wanted a big family, and so they both got pregnant, twice each, first Sam and then Lisa, using the same donor for all of the pregnancies. Since one of the pregnancies resulted in twins, they now have five children, ranging in age from seven to sixteen.

About ten years ago Sam began to read about men transitioning to become the women they knew themselves to be on the inside. Then he heard about a woman who had transitioned to become a man. He researched; he learned more. And he realized that this was the secret he had kept his whole life; finally, he knew who he was.

He was afraid to tell Lisa. He hinted for a while. She knew he was reading about trans men. She did not have a major adverse reaction when he finally came clean. She listened and tried to understand. Mostly she was scared that something bad would happen to their family. They could both imagine the horror of hate crimes, of having media camped out on their lawn.

Sam and Lisa have moved forward together. With hormones and upper surgery (Sam also had a hysterectomy), it didn't take very long until Sam stopped looking like a female. Lisa confesses that she was always attracted to his male energy, so it's not as if he has changed into someone she can't recognize. It's really only when they look at old photos that she sees just how much he has changed; then it's like looking at pictures of children as they grow up; you can really see the difference. Lower surgery is next on the agenda, and it will require a month at a hospital in Chicago. But the most crucial measures of the transition have already been completed. With or without more surgeries, Sam now recognizes himself.

Sam, who is an athletics director for a school, recently gave a talk about his decision to transition. The following has been edited for print:

As early as the age of six I became aware of feeling uncomfortable with my female body. The image I saw in the mirror and the image I knew others saw when they looked at me did not jibe with the way I felt. I loved dressing as a boy. I had one older brother and two younger ones, and I wanted to be like them. Despite the feminine outfits and dresses that my mother purchased for me, I kept digging out my older brother's hand-me-downs. At the age of seven, I pleaded with Mom until she took me to get my long, wavy hair cut very short.

I preferred to play with boys. I was envious of the trucks and cars my brothers possessed. I especially wanted the really cool Evel Knievel motorcycle toy that you cranked up and let go and watched as it made daredevil leaps over various obstacles. It was dynamic and exciting. When my parents went away on trips and brought back gifts for us, I was usually given a doll. Because I never wanted to disappoint my parents or hurt their feelings, I held back the tears. It was the same when my birthday came along; I didn't like "girl toys." In fact, I looked forward to my brothers' birthdays more than my own.

I was told I was a tomboy. I accepted this label because there were no other options in the 1970s. And at least it had the word "boy" in it.

When I was eight years old, I wanted to play football, baseball, ice hockey, and all the other sports that were available to my older brother. But with no Title IX (the education amendment which states that no person shall be excluded, based on gender, from programs or activities receiving federal assistance) in effect yet, there were very few programs for girls. I was lucky, though. My dad was involved with youth sports, and he saw that his daughter was a very good athlete. He was supportive and wanted me to get involved. I remember him going to a town meeting and standing up and saying that girls should be able to play baseball at least, since it was a noncontact sport, with boys, or have a league of their own. The battle he fought was not popular at the time; it was considered unsafe for girls to play with the boys, contact or not. Really? They could get hurt? How? Were they more fragile? Weaker bones or something like that? When Dad said he would take me on his team, the other coaches did not fight him.

I played Little League baseball with the boys for five years. By the time I was eleven I was one of the better players and was therefore liked and respected by the other team members, who only wanted to win. When I got up to bat, opposing players would often question whether I was male or female. Even after hearing the "Let's go, Sue," chants from my team's bench, they would still argue about whether I was a boy or a girl. The disconnect was evident: my name did not match their perception of me. I was always mistaken for a boy—whether it was in sports settings or other environments. Sure, I was teased a bit, but I didn't care, especially when I got up to bat and hit a ball into the outfield and ran around the bases with an ear-to-ear grin. Sports was the perfect arena for me to build self-esteem. It also camouflaged many of the emotional challenges that I was battling.

At age twelve I made the All-Star team, the members of which were honored at an end-of-season banquet. My parents were adamant that I wear a dress to the event. They were proud and wanted everyone to know that their All Star was a girl. I did not want to disappoint them, but I didn't want to wear a dress either. I cried for days and weeks leading up to the banquet. Though it was absolute torture for me, I wore the dress. In the end it was nothing compared to what was coming my way next: puberty.

My body started to change—slowly. Puberty is not generally easy for anyone, but most can embrace it on some level. While all my friends who were girls could not wait to get their first bras or their periods, I was praying that someone up there would hear me and I would never get my period. It made me sick inside to hear adults tell girls who had begun to menstruate that they were "young women now." More importantly, I prayed I would not grow breasts. I liked to walk around shirtless, and that would not go over well with breasts. What was wrong with me?

I had to keep these feelings to myself. Since they didn't make sense even to me, I felt shame. There were not a lot of resources back then. We didn't have the internet, or any role models, or even school counselors who could help. Parenting theory, which is more or less generational, did not provide any answers. There wasn't a language to even describe gender variance, or if there was, it was not something that was shared or discussed in the circles I traveled in. When I got my period, I was angry. I hated it; I especially hated the "you're a woman now" comments that came from a few older relatives. My mom might have said that too. Shopping for my first bra was ridiculously embarrassing and humiliating for me.

I was so uncomfortable with my body. I was slender, and even though I was small chested, the growths there did not feel like they belonged. In fact when they first invented sports bras, that's what I got—and I never owned anything different.

Tight sports bras, to help make me flatter. That was doable for the time being.

Being a teenager and feeling really different definitely made life more challenging.

It was easier to conform than fight. My days of looking and being mistaken as a boy were fading into the past. It seemed inevitable that I would grow up and be a girl.

As I entered high school, I shifted from questioning my gender to questioning my sexuality. Who was I attracted to? Social pressure is huge. I say this with great empathy as I think of my own two teenage daughters—who are sixteen and fourteen now. I wanted to fit in and be normal. My daughters feel this way every day. I had boyfriends—sort of. I ran for the hills if things started to get too serious. I had my "crushes" on Fonzie and Leif Garrett. I tried to grow my hair. I tried to dress more femininely. But never, ever did it feel like I fit in.

Athletics saved me once again. Society "allows" girls in sports to be more masculine (by "masculine," I mean aggressive, athletic, strong, mentally and physically tough). On the playing field, I could be all of these and it was OK. My friends referred to me as a jock, an athlete, a tomboy—all of which were acceptable terms. But there was also a stereotype for girls like me, some of whom were called lesbians or dykes. Sexual attraction has nothing to do with whether someone likes sports, is good at sports, or exhibits "masculine" qualities. But stereotypes are strong and impactful in our culture. During high school I had strong suspicions—all based on the norms of the time—that I could be gay. I tried very hard to prove I was not a lesbian.

There was a lot of homophobia back then, and identifying as gay or lesbian was considered weird, strange, perverted—not normal. People my age made fun of gay people. Adults too sometimes made negative comments (direct and indirect) about gay or lesbian people. I would tell myself over and over, "I can't be a lesbian! It's not OK; my life will be ruined." But it remained the only way to make sense of my feelings. I began accepting that this was what I was. I was attracted to women. I still felt tomboyish, and I had incredible dysphoria regarding my female anatomy. But I had no other label to define myself, no other way to feel like I somehow "fit in." I had friends who were lesbians, and we shared some similarities.

I came out to my family and friends as a lesbian when I was twenty-two years old. I never felt at peace with my revelation, maybe because I knew deep down inside that it was not accurate and didn't really describe who I was or how I felt. I did not see any other options.

After college I met my wife, Lisa. We had a beautiful commitment ceremony up in the scenic mountains of New Hampshire years before gay marriage was legalized. We invited many of our friends and family. Lisa dressed in typical white bridal dress. Although I wish I had been brave enough to wear a tuxedo or suit and tie, ironically, I felt I had to conform to the norm that maintained that we were both brides. I settled for a navy-blue, suit-style dress. After all, lesbians were not women trying to be men; they were women—albeit some more masculine than others—and to be frank, it was frowned upon for a lesbian to try to be like a man. At least that was the message I seemed to get.

I continued to live under the dark cloud of not feeling right in my body. The issue became especially critical when I considered whether or not to have a baby.

This is a subject Lisa and I discussed often. We knew we wanted children, and it was just assumed that Lisa was going to be the baby maker. I never wanted to be pregnant, never envisioned or dreamed about it. Not me. No way.

When I turned thirty-one, my feelings changed. Lisa wasn't ready to get pregnant herself; she was working toward her MBA and had a very busy work schedule. Although somewhat shocked and surprised, she did not want to stand in my way when I told her I was ready to do it.

Not only did we want children, but I thought being pregnant might finally make me feel more like a woman. Women have babies; I needed to do this. Much to my surprise, being pregnant was not so bad. We were so excited to bring a child into our family. Estrogen and pregnancy hormones filled me with both maternal instincts and feelings of femininity. It was as if a faucet was turned on, or maybe a hose. I felt confident that having a baby was going to change me and make me feel more like a woman is supposed to feel.

The most magnificent thing that ever happened to me and our family was the birth of my daughter. And wanting a sibling for her who would be close in age, I became pregnant with our second daughter, who was born two years later. But although getting pregnant was the best decision I ever made because of its results, my girls, it did not change me, except that I became a better person in many ways. But there was no change regarding my feelings about my gender. Lisa gave birth to our first son, who is eight, and the twins, who are six. Being so busy with jobs, children, and many other responsibilities did not leave a lot of time to think about myself.

My life felt pretty normal, until three events got me rethinking about who I am.

1. *We had a sitter who took care of the twins occasionally, when they were just infants. She was a student*

at Wellesley College. She asked me one day if I would mind answering some questions for a project she was doing in a women's studies class. I agreed. The questions—which concerned womanhood, femaleness, feminism, etc.—got me rethinking/questioning who I was at the core.

2. *Around the same time I heard about this man who'd had a baby. I'd never heard anything like that before. He was going to be on* Oprah. *I wrote down the time and day and made sure to tape the show. Then I watched it in secret. I kind of knew I was brushing against the tip of an iceberg, but my intense curiosity overcame my apprehension. The man was Thomas Beatie, a trans man who had had surgeries to help him become physically who he knew himself to be on the inside. I told myself I just needed to keep busy and not think about how alike we were. The idea of me transitioning still seemed ridiculous. I would lose everything I had; it wasn't worth the havoc it was certain to create in my life.*

3. *Then there was Chaz Bono, who also came out publically as a trans man. He wrote a book called* Transition: Becoming Who I Was Always Meant to Be. *I remembered him well from the Sonny and Cher show. Back then he was Chastity, a cute little girl. I read his book and then read everything I could about him. The more I learned the more I realized that this was what I might be. But what was I going to do about it? Nothing.*

"Nothing" only lasted a day. After these revelations, I realized I needed to put some focus on myself. It was time

to finally answer those questions that had been haunting me since childhood. I began reading and researching everything I could on transsexualism.

After a lot of research, therapy, and introspection, I came to the conclusion that I was not comfortable identifying as a female anymore—and I decided to take very small steps toward transitioning. It was scary. I remember attending a monthly transgender group. We sat in a large circle, maybe thirty of us. Thirty people; that's a lot. I had thought I was the only one in Massachusetts to feel this way. We were all different, but all united in that we all knew on some level that we were not women, regardless of the physical characteristics we had at birth. I asked a question to the group: "How did you do it? How did you get the courage?"

I was so overwhelmed with what needed to happen and with the order it had to happen in. Even more overwhelming was the question of how I would tell people. One of the guys said to me, "I know it's scary, but you have to tackle it brick by brick." That advice really stood out for me. I was afraid I would lose my wife, my kids, my job, my family, and friends. I was in my midforties; I was afraid I would alienate myself. I imagined negative responses from everyone I knew. Part of me thought I was weird. The other part knew I would have to get past that notion. First and foremost, I needed to accept and love myself. That would be the first brick, and it was a big one.

My transition began two and a half years ago (as of this writing). I did not come out publically right away. I had to tell my wife. I had to know she would be OK with it. I needed her unconditional love. But this would be a challenge for her too. While she never turned her back on me or showed me any less love or respect, she needed to sort through her own feelings about the situation.

My first official physical change was top surgery. It was a huge relief and in some ways marked the beginning of my transition as it helped me to feel better in my body. Hormone treatments started six months later, low doses of testosterone resulting in gradual changes, none of which could be noticed very easily, if at all, by the people I came into contact with daily. This made it much easier on my family. I had time to talk with each of my kids, modifying my narrative so that it was always age (and individual) appropriate. While I changed very slowly, I made videos each week for the first year and a half. My kids will tell you that they noticed very little change, until they see an old picture or an early video.

After taking care of my family, the next big brick was to share what was going on with me in the professional world. I decided to talk to my supervisor. Since I was pretty sure he had no idea what I wanted to talk to him about, I prefaced our meeting by saying that the subject was personal and I would prefer not to speak to him in any of the offices or classrooms in the school where we both work.

We sat on a park bench down the street from the school. I was very nervous, but I trusted him and my gut told me he would understand. I'd picked up sandwiches, but I wasn't planning on eating mine. I had practiced and rehearsed what I would say, but sure enough, I beat around the bush anyway. It seemed to take hours to spit the out the words. I think I was hoping he would guess and say them for me.

His response, when I did finally managed to tell him my story, was warm, compassionate, and understanding. My fears were put to rest. What a relief. From that day forward a really special and unique bond formed between us, and I will always cherish it.

The next concern was how to best communicate my transition to the community. Many letters, including one from me, were sent out to parents of the young people attending my school and also the community at large. The support, much of which came mostly via email, was amazing. People said they were proud of me; they saw me as courageous. Their understanding gave me such hope and inspiration—not just for myself but for humankind.

Changing my name was a large step in the process. Sometimes I think my brain has not caught up completely to other changes. I pass 100 percent now, but during the first year there were times when I was misgendered (identified as female). As one trangender individual once said to me early on, "You can't run from your past."

I am fortunate to still have the parts of my past that mean the most to me; I did not relocate or change jobs, and I remain happily married to Lisa. Most people know me as Sam, the individual who transitioned. They respect my privacy and don't usually ask questions. While I'm happy to talk about my transition when the opportunity presents itself, I don't want it to be the only thing that defines me. But I do feel a responsibility to help educate people on the facts. There are a lot of trans folks out there who are treated poorly and have not been nearly as fortunate as I have been. Everyone's journey is different.

Two and a half years later, I am at peace. I am still changing, which is kind of strange, like going through puberty in my forties. My wife has been very supportive and still loves me for all that I am (and still gets annoyed with me about the same things that annoyed her before I transitioned). My kids have been great. My daughter, who is now sixteen, gave her ninth grade talk on the subject of being true to oneself. She used me as a role model and example.

My transition has helped me become a better person, a more compassionate and kind individual, and a happier man. In fact, I am the man I was always meant to be.

Michelle

You Can't Keep a Secret Forever

For the first ten years of her life, Michelle didn't give her gender identity much thought. But as she got older she began to note that boys and girls reacted differently to various situations—and she couldn't help noticing that her reactions were more in line with those of the girls she knew. She didn't "feel" the way she thought boys felt based on their behavior. And when she got to the age when kids begin thinking about clothes, she realized that she liked the way girls dressed and the way they styled their hair—and she didn't care for the way boys looked at all.

Michelle, who is sixty-three as of this writing, came of age in the 1960s, when you didn't dare talk to anyone about these sorts of observations if you didn't want to wind up in an institution. So she kept her feelings to herself. And while she played some sports (though never at the league level) and she passed well enough as a boy, her insecurities and confusion (there weren't better words back then to express what she felt) kept her from making many friends.

As an only child, there were no siblings looking over her shoulder. And her parents, both of whom worked, didn't seem to notice there were any problems either, though Michelle supposed her mother must have had an inkling and simply chose not to mention it back then. "You can't keep a secret forever," she says. "You make a mistake, fail to put something back the right way in the right drawer . . ." Michelle started to wear her mother's clothes, shoes, and makeup as soon as she got home from school. Looking in the mirror, she felt good.

Michelle dated a few girls as a teen, the first of whom she really liked. She and "L" kissed, hugged, and held hands. But when L, who was Jewish, told her parents about the boy she was dating, her parents explained that she wasn't allowed to date outside of their faith. L argued with them for a full week to no avail. Eventually L told Michelle she was sorry, but she could not disobey her parents; they had to end their relationship. The other girls Michelle dated did nothing for her. Nor was she attracted to boys. Observing other couples making out led her to believe that during her make-out sessions she acted more the part of the woman than that of the man. She only became more confused during these years, and hence more of a loner. Friendships began, then ended. Nothing stuck. She wanted to understand what was wrong with her, but there was absolutely nowhere to go with her questions.

Like the majority of her peers, Michelle was not that interested in school. She was an average student who held a variety of part-time jobs throughout her high school years. Her father was willing to put her through college, but she preferred to continue working. Though she daydreamed about what it would be like to be a cocktail waitress or to wear a beautiful wedding dress (for the feel of it; not because she wanted to get married), she worked overseeing stock for a company that made dials and pressure gauges.

When she was younger, she'd enjoyed collecting coins and stamps. One day when she was in her twenties, she walked into a coin and jewelry store to have a look around, and she struck up a conversation with a young man working there. Before she knew it, they'd become friends and she was working there herself. After about five years, she and her coworker bought out the owner of the company. And five years after that, Michelle, who disliked the long days that were part and parcel of being a business owner, sold out to her partner and went to work for other people she knew in the same business.

In all this time Michelle had never married. She'd thought about it; she'd had a few relationships with women, but they hadn't really worked out. Even kissing women left her wondering, *Is this all there is?* Now of course she knows her lack of interest was a component of her gender dysphoria, but back then she still didn't have a name for what she perceived to be her shortcomings.

One day, Michelle decided to wear lipstick into the salon where she went regularly to get her hair cut. The hairdresser was kind, and Michelle thought she would be understanding. She was also wearing women's underwear under her street clothes, so she went in "feeling" like a woman. She was getting bolder. Her mother and aunt had been with her a couple of times when she'd worn lipstick. They were really the only two people, prior to the hairdresser, who understood Michelle's inclinations. They agreed that since she wasn't doing any harm to anyone, she shouldn't have to feel bad about wanting to express herself in that way.

Michelle eventually ended her career in the coin and jewelry business to take care of her mother. Her father had been out of the picture for some sixteen years by then. He had become diabetic years earlier and eventually developed gangrene in one leg and had to have it amputated. Although he had a brother helping to care for him, he couldn't tolerate his situation and eventually ended it by hanging himself. (When Michelle heard the news and rushed home, she found her uncle, the one who had been her father's part-time caretaker, rifling through her father's drawers. When she asked what was going on, her uncle, who was a Jehovah's Witness minister, told her to "fuck off." Later she would learn that he had withdrawn a large sum of money from her father's bank account, which he had access to because he'd once helped Michelle's father to pay his bills. This was money that was supposed to go to Michelle with the rest of her father's estate.)

In 1995, Michelle's mother was alone, eighty-five years old, and sickly following breast cancer and a mastectomy. A visiting nurse came in to administer to Michelle's mom's medical needs daily, but Michelle did the cooking, cleaning, bill paying, and all the other tasks her mother could no longer see to. Ironically, Michelle had never learned domestic tasks; as a well-loved only child, her mother had always done everything for her. But now the situation was reversed, and she quickly taught herself to take over. While she had never really gotten along with her father, she adored her mom and was happy to be her caretaker. She devoted herself to her mother's wellbeing for eight years, until her mother's health declined to the point where she needed more care than Michelle and a visiting nurse could provide and had to be placed in a nursing home. Still, Michelle continued with her routine, visiting her mother seven days a week, morning and night. These were hard times. By then her mother was unable to speak and was showing signs of dementia. Michelle tried to communicate with her but never knew whether her mother understood any of what she said. In April of 2004, after about eight months in the nursing home, Michelle's mom passed on.

Looking for answers to the many questions that life had thrown her way, Michelle returned to the Albanian Orthodox church where she had been baptized years earlier. She also began working for the church, doing maintenance and repairs. Because she had never had reason to learn to use a computer, she still knew very little about transgender issues, and in fact she had never come across the word "transgender." "Transvestite" was the closest she'd managed, but that didn't encompass the scope of what she was feeling.

It is only in the last few years that Michelle has come to learn more about who she really is and what kinds of options are available to her. She has begun seeing the appropriate doctors and has started hormone therapy and also electrolysis and is working toward feminizing her voice. This has resulted in her learning about various social groups and agencies. Suddenly the world is a different place, opening its arms to her and inviting her to enjoy her life as a woman, to the extent that she is able. She relates that she is still a virgin and is unlikely to want to make changes in that department.

Michelle retired from her work at the church when she decided to come out and transition from male to female. She felt certain the church would not be able to tolerate the changes she was going through and the ones that lay ahead. One of her concerns was which bathroom she would use. Technically, she wasn't allowed to use either one. The only option she believed she had was to leave the premises and go to a local business to use their bathroom. She felt she could no longer remain a member of the congregation either.

One year after coming out, the priest from Michelle's church, who by then had learned of her transition, called her to say the congregation missed her and the church wanted her to come back to work. She had missed the people and the work too and was happy to return. The bathrooms were no longer an issue either. She was told she could use the office bathroom.

Michelle is living her life as a woman now. She doesn't know what the future will bring. Because of her age and her financial situation—and, to be honest, her insecurities—she will not undergo sex reassignment surgery. While the changes she is working on may seem only preliminary to others, to Michelle they are highly significant. They have changed her life and the way she feels about herself.

She has noticed that people are more helpful to her now that she presents as a woman; they are kinder than they ever were before. The men at her church were friendlier before she transitioned and afterward were a bit a little standoffish, but they continue to be as considerate as ever. Perhaps people recognize her as someone who is living her life authentically. Already she knows that deciding to make her transition was the best decision she has ever made. She feels good, "really good."

Her ultimate goal is to get to a place where she can be helpful to younger transgender individuals. She wants to let them know that they are not alone, that their situation is not hopeless. She wants to bring them comfort and listen to their stories and share her own story of keeping her secret for so long. She herself never attempted suicide, but it did cross her mind plenty of times, especially after her father chose that method to deal with his challenges. She wants to make sure the younger transgender people she hopes to know in the future will never see ending their lives as the better (or only) option.

From Linda's Office

When Michelle first came to me she was already in her sixties, and her facial hair had gone gray and white. Therefore, she was unable to undergo laser hair removal. Her full face is being done the old-fashioned way, through electrolysis. If she had come out when she was younger, her hair would have still been dark, and we could have used the laser.

Because the response to transgender issues has been so much more tolerant in recent times, many male-to-female transgender people are coming out before they even reach puberty. These young people may never need electrolysis *or* laser work on their faces, because they will receive hormone blockers from their physicians that will keep them from ever growing beards and may reduce their body hair. This growing hair issue depends on many variations, including the hormone treatment regime prescribed by their doctors.

As of this writing Michelle has had about ninety hours of electrolysis over the past two years (at $95 an hour, she's spent $8,550). (Prices of course vary state to state and region to region.) Her beard is almost gone. It should take about another ten hours, for a total of one hundred hours, to completely re- move her beard. As an electrologist, I am able to remove about eight hundred to nine hundred hairs per hour. This may vary from one electrologist to another and the modality of electrolysis they use. Michelle will spend about $9,500 when all is said and done.

On a personal note, Michelle and I have become friends over the many hours we have worked together. I have a sister who had suffered from MSA, Multiple System Atrophy (a cousin of Parkinson's), and whom I visited weekly, on my day off. Michelle, who is a natural caretaker, came with me almost every week. Her willingness to help with domestic tasks as well as to join in on conversations is a testament to her beautiful nature.

FAQs

FAQ: What exactly does SRS involve?

For MTF (male-to-female) transition, SRS means the removal of the testes and refashioning of the penis (or sometimes part of the bowel) to create a vagina. The urethra is shortened, and the clitoris is formed from part of the glans of the penis. For FTM (female-to-male), SRS can include breast reductions (mastectomies) and removal of the ovaries, uterus, and vaginal lining (hysterectomy), along with a closing of the vagina. It is then possible to construct a penis from the muscle tissue and a clitoris that has been enlarged as a result of hormone therapy.

FAQ: What is labiaplasty?

The labiaplasty is the second part of a two-stage vaginoplasty, where labia and a clitoral hood are created. This is often performed a few months after the first part of the procedure. In some cases, labiaplasty is an elective procedure to improve appearance after a one-stage vaginoplasty.

FAQ: What is a vaginal deepening procedure?

In a vaginal deepening procedure (VDP), grafted skin from either the surgical site or the lower abdomen is used to deepen the vagina by dissecting along the vaginal plane previously established, then packing the region and utilizing the original vaginal lining to heal after packing is removed.

FAQ: What is orchiectomy?

Orchiectomy is the surgical removal of one or both testicles to lower one's level of testosterone.

FAQ: What is a tracheal shave?

A tracheal shave is a procedure in which the thyroid cartilage (or the Adam's apple, which can be a telltale sign of a male history) is reduced in size. It is often performed as a component of facial feminizing surgery (FFS). But it can be performed at the time of the SRS if desired. (Note: if the doctor takes off too much the patient can risk using their voice.)

FAQ: Is it over once you leave the hospital?

In the case of male-to-female SRS, some patients may need to wear a catheter home because things aren't fully healed. The plumbing has been rerouted, and the urethra is in a new place. But even for those who do need a catheter, once it is removed it's amazing to see how well the bladder functions with its new apparatus.

FAQ: Is there potential for complications resulting from SRS?

Any surgery can result in complications, and SRS is no exception. Following is a partial list of possible complications:

- Death: Death is always a possible outcome for almost any kind of surgery, although I personally have never heard of anyone dying from SRS. Most doctors take extensive precautionary measures to make sure each patient is healthy enough for the procedures.
- Need for multiple surgeries: I have seen a few people go back for up to four surgeries, because patients try to do too much too soon and/or because of various medical reasons.

- Fistula: A fistula is abnormal connection between organs. In the case of SRS, a fistula or an aperture can occur between the vagina and the colon.
- Blood loss: As in any surgery, hemorrhaging, necessitating donor blood units, can occur. As mentioned above, avoidance of certain drugs, vitamins, and prescription hormones before surgery can help reduce the risk of blood loss. (One of my clients did lose blood and went into shock; the doctors brought her back.)
- Blood clots: Here, too, avoiding drugs, vitamins, and hormones can lessen the chance of clots. Quitting smoking, exercising, and weight reduction (for those who are overweight) can also help to reduce the risk of clots. Blood clots can lead to strokes, heart attacks, and even paralysis. (Many endocrinologists, physicians, and therapists refuse to start hormone therapy for individuals until they have stopped smoking.)
- Pneumonia: Fluid in the lungs, as most of us know, is another common result of surgery. Quitting smoking, increasing exercise, and reducing weight before surgery can help reduce the risk of pneumonia. After surgery, most doctors will suggest movement—sitting up, walking to the bathroom—as soon as possible.
- Allergic reactions: To avoid the chance of allergic reactions as much as possible, patients should inform anesthesiologists and other medical team members of any allergies that they have experienced in the past—especially to drugs such as penicillin.
- Infection: The best way to avoid post-op infections is to follow medical team directives to a T, especially those regarding vaginal dilation and hygiene.
- Necrosis: Necrosis is the death of tissue, and it can be caused by infection or by tissue rejection, or even by loss of blood supply.

- Vaginal collapse: Like the other complications listed above, vaginal collapse does not result from SRS alone. Biological women can experience vaginal collapse when parts of the vaginal support network "relax," causing less stability for the pelvic organs. Of course vaginal collapse is of special concern to trans women having SRS, who can experience this outcome as a result of the shrinking of skin graft inside the vagina. Properly performed dilation techniques can reduce the risks of vaginal collapse.

- Excretory reactions: Bowel problems—especially in cases when the patient has experienced a fistula—and urinary problems can result from SRS. Urinary problems can range from inappropriate stream direction to pain during urination to incontinence.

- Sexual performance: The greater number of SRS patients report that they are able to have healthy sex lives postsurgery. In fact, SRS often enhances the libidos of trans women because they are finally free to experience sex from within the body they have always wanted. For many, "losing their virginity" becomes a goal, something to get behind them. Once they know they can really achieve an orgasm, they can move forward in their relationships. However, there are some who are no longer able to experience orgasm after SRS. A vagina that is too shallow, too narrow, or too sensitive can be the cause. Numbness of the genitals can also inhibit organism. Most (but certainly not all) trans women require some amount of lubrication before penetrative sexual activity. It may take some experimenting—and some time—to get things going.

- Psychological: We won't say too much about the psychological risks here because we believe that in most cases, when the rules have been followed and SRS trans women spend the right amount of time living full time as women (at least one year) and see the therapist and endocrinologist (and don't forget the hair-removal pros) as recommended, the psychological risks (depression, regret) of SRS will be negligible. But that's why we've collected the stories in this book, so that you can see for yourself what kind of psychological outcomes most people have.

It's worth noting once again that most SRS surgeries are done by top surgeons who have high success rates. These excellent surgeons will be onboard post-op to make sure everything is going the way it should. Then it is up to the patient to follow the rules regarding hygiene, dilation, etc., and to let the medical team know immediately if any potential problems arise.

People who travel out of state (or out of country) for surgery will want to stay in the location where their surgery is performed even after they are released from the hospital, in case there are any problems. In some cases they may stay as long as month to offset complications. If they are staying in town, they may want to bring along a friend or relative who can tend to them as they rest in their hotel room. If they have flown to their SRS destination, they will also want to arrange for wheelchairs at both ends of their flight home. Unless they are able to stay in town for the full extent of their recovery, they will need to line up post-op medical care *before* their SRS. All SRS patients will need to purchase sanitary pads, panty liners, disinfectant, baby wipes, and lubricants ahead of time too. Vitamin E capsules are also good to have on hand as vitamin E increases healing rates and helps reduce scarring.

Just as important as having the right supplies on hand is giving the body a chance to rest after all it has been through.

People who feel they must jump right back into their old work routines are putting themselves at risk, and they shouldn't even think of doing any heavy lifting for a good long time. It will probably take about six weeks just for the superficial swelling from SRS to go down. Less superficial aspects of the surgery will take even longer to heal. Fluid discharges, sloughing skin or tissue, and hemorrhoid flare-ups (for those who are prone to hemorrhoids, at least) can all add to the general discomfort of those first weeks. Also, there will be hormone level changes and maybe some mood swings as patients adjust. Emotions (laughter as well as tears) can come to the surface during this time. These reactions are all to be expected.

FAQ: What hormone therapy regime is typical for male-to-female transitions?

Physicians, endocrinologists, or health-care providers may prescribe any of the following: estrogen, a testosterone blocker (spironolactone), and/or progesterone. Note that your provider may consider dihydrotestosterone if your body has a reaction to the stronger spironolactone.

From Linda's Office

Rona was eighteen when she came in for hair removal. She spent between $1,200 and $1,300, mostly all for laser work but with one treatment for electrolysis, over a period of five months preceding her SRS. Knowing she wanted to transition but also knowing doctors would not offer her SRS until she reached the age of eighteen, she had started on testosterone blockers (spironolactone) and an estrogen product (estradiol) around puberty and thus had no facial hair and required no work on face or neck.

FAQ: What hormone therapy regime is typical for female-to-male transition?

Testosterone is prescribed to induce masculinity. Finasteride and dutasteride are medicines which stop the production of dihydrotestosterone, a specific form of testosterone blocker that has action on the skin, hair, and prostate.

Of course, all dosages for hormone therapy medicine should be determined by a health-care professional in light of any given transgender individual's blood levels. It is important for these blood levels to be checked regularly. In some cases, hormone blood levels may be high or low, requiring an adjustment of their dosage.

FAQ: Are hormones available over the internet?

Just about everything is available over the internet, but not everything should be. Hormone levels vary for biological women, spiking during menstruation and falling off during menopause, etc. The levels of hormones for a trans woman need to be regulated by a doctor, since her body will not be equipped to regulate hormones on its own.

One trans woman I knew in the '90s, let's call her J, decided to "do it herself" and began taking hormones without the guidance of a physician. Like so many others at that time, she was nowhere near ready to come out to friends and families, but she thought she could at least soften her skin and reduce her beard and thus find some relief for herself. She bought her hormones over the internet. They were shipped to her from another country for prices far less than what she would have paid if she were seeing an endocrinologist and getting prescriptions from her/him. Back then it wasn't easy to get prescriptions for hormone therapy, even if you wanted to. While she had done her homework and knew how much of a dosage she should be taking, the product itself was not regulated and didn't always conform to the dosage amounts listed on the labels.

J was only in her forties when she had a severe heart attack. The doctors who cared for her in the hospital discovered that her hormone levels were almost three times higher than they should have been. As a result, her body had gone into shock.

J *did* survive, but it required having open-heart surgery. She learned her lesson, however. She has completed her transition under the care of an endocrinologist. Her doctor monitors her hormone levels regularly and determines when dosages can be increased and at what levels.

Other conditions that can be caused by improper dosages of hormones include but are not limited to: gall bladder stones, thrombosis (blood clots), and liver damage.

Regular blood work is required to check hormone levels and to avoid risks and complications.

Note: When preparing for SRS, patients are asked to stop taking hormones (along with many prescription drugs and even vitamins) for three weeks (approximately) before surgery. As with any surgery, this is done to reduce the chance of excessive bleeding or blood clots. Many patients are afraid to go off hormones. Often they've found emotional comfort through balanced hormone levels. Trans women are afraid a resurgence of testosterone will stimulate male attributes they hoped never to experience again. It can also lead to mood swings and even depression. Knowing what to expect and knowing that it is only temporary can help ease their distress.

From Linda's Office

Rita was twenty-five when she came for hair removal. She had dark hair and a lighter skin tone and was also on estradiol and spironolactone, which, again, help to reduce the frequency of facial hair *in most cases*. Rita didn't need electrolysis on her face, but she wanted it on her eyebrows. She did have full-facial laser, including the removal of hair on the outer edge of nostrils. (Hair removal professionals are not permitted to remove hair from *inside* the nose). She underwent twelve full-face treatments for $2,400 and two perioral treatments (above and below the lips) for $200 for a total of $2,600. In addition was the work on her eyebrows, at $745, for a final total of $3,345.

Rita came in twice a month for the first two months, then once a month for the next three. Thereafter we skipped to every other month and eventually to every two to three months. After several laser visits it's a good idea to evaluate what's happening by letting the hair grow out so you can see what's left. Rita's beard was gradually disappearing with ten visits over the course of one year. She needed four more visits, two more for full-face work and two for perioral work, to complete the job. All told the process took about a year and a half.

Rita's work was inexpensive because she started so young. The combination of her particular genetic makeup and the hormones she took meant she didn't even need to have any work done on her body.

Rita's decision to have electrolysis on her eyebrows came from a fear that they would wind up too thin if she tried to pluck them herself. Also, she wanted a permanent fix, which waxing or plucking doesn't provide. She wanted her brows to look full and natural but to be clean. She also wanted work done on the glabella (the area between the brows). Her brows required twelve clearings (or 6.75 hours, 405 minutes), spread out the year and a half she was with us.

FAQ: What do SRS surgeons require before they will schedule a surgery?

Generally, surgeons must receive referral letters from two different therapists at least two months prior to the surgery date. One of these therapists must be an MD or PhD. The second letter may be from a licensed clinical social worker or a master's-level therapist. Both letter writers must have specialized training in the treatment of gender dysphoria. In addition, a letter of introduction from one of the patient's therapists stating that the patient is in the process of transitioning is required before the surgery can take place. Surgeons will confirm the validity of the letters. This is in accordance with the World Professional Association for Transgender Health (WPATH—formerly known as Harry Benjamin Standards of Care).

FAQ: Are there reproductive options for trans women?

Some men, before transitioning, preserve sperm in a sperm bank in case they want children down the line.

FAQ: Can trans women have orgasms?

Yes, in most cases, transgender women who have undergone sex reassignment surgery can have orgasms. Dr. Toby Meltzer, one of the top doctors in the country performing this kind of surgery (he's extremely talented and has performed thousands of SRSes), tells us that if the individual was able to have satisfying sex before the surgery, they are more than likely to be able to have it afterward. This is because the sensitive part of the penis has been used in the formation of the new clitoris. But in order to guarantee the best results, it's important for trans women to take their time and choose the best doctors, from their endocrinologist to their surgeons, even if it means delaying transitions to wait for appointments with busy physicians.

One client of mine rushed through everything. She didn't follow the protocol that her therapist laid out for her. She managed to manipulate various doctors into putting their signatures on the paperwork she needed in order to have surgery before she should have. She chose the first doctor who accepted her, was affordable, and could do the SRS very quickly. As a result, she hasn't had an orgasm since her surgery, a few years ago now.

Some SRS doctors, such as well-known physician Dr. Marci Bowers, are so busy there can be a two-year waiting period for the initial surgery. For transfeminine bottom surgeries, some doctors perform two procedures. There may be a dozen SRS doctors in the United States. There are also some in Canada, Thailand, Serbia, and Belgium. People in the transgender community talk to one another; word gets around. They rely on each other's experiences to determine the best medical options. They also know who to go to if they feel they can't wait too long. In most cases after a successful SRS, you can't tell the difference between the vagina of a transgender woman and a biological one.

From Linda's Office

Jane has been with us over a nine-year period. She began her treatments at age forty-nine. Jane wanted to move slowly because she planned to transition slowly; she also wanted to be able to work within the confines of her budget. She underwent ninety electrolysis treatments for a cost of about $6,000. These occurred over 77 hours, or 4,620 minutes.

Jane also had laser work done, on her chest, abs, and in the Brazilian zone. This required another 25 hours spread out over thirty treatments at the cost of about $6,470. All together her 102 hours of laser hair removal and electrolysis cost her approximately $12,470.

D

D, who is just short of twenty-five, has always presented as feminine. Even as a kid she never felt the need to hide behind a false persona. Part of this may have been because of her relationship with her mom, who was liberal in her thinking, protective of D, and always available to sit with her and watch shows that explored gender issues. In fact, her mom's favorite movie was *Transamerica*, a 2005 independent dramedy about a transgender woman on a road trip with her long-lost son.

This is not to say that D and her mom talked extensively about D's issues. Until D was twenty-two, she didn't even really comprehend what it meant to be transgender. She simply was what she was, and her mother's understanding of her was inclusive. Once, when D was about fourteen, her mom asked her if she ever worried that she would be mistaken for a girl, and D answered that she wasn't sure. For the most part, though, neither of them felt the need to dissect D's uniqueness with words. Her mother was more concerned about D's safety, afraid that she could easily become a target of violence, but she was never disapproving of her androgyny.

But D's self-possession does not mean that she hasn't taken her share of abuse over the years. In fact, she suffered severe bullying in middle school and the first year of high school. Making matters worse, puberty for D was a violent and unnatural process. Rather than stay put and take the ongoing mistreatment she experienced, D switched schools. And when that didn't work, she dropped out of high school. She never felt that conforming to meet the conventional standards of others was the right solution. Dressing differently, she knew, would not make the problem go away. As for her education, D, always an A student, would eventually wrap up her GREs, excel on her SATs, and graduate with honors from college with a degree in art, specializing in textiles.

D can't remember a time when she didn't think of herself as being female. Accordingly, she didn't have the kind of "coming out" experience that people who have long lived in denial often have as they first learn to accept themselves and then gear up to make the announcement to their loved ones. She knew she wanted to live as a woman and that that was an option she could satisfy, but she didn't feel it *had* to happen until she was about twenty-two. At that time she realized she wanted to be in the body she needed and wanted, not the one she had. Her transition—aided by hormones and hair removal—was the most natural progression in the world.

Unfortunately, D's mother never got to witness her transition. She died three years ago at the age of fifty-one after several surgeries and a long struggle with uterine cancer. Her death was devastating for D. D's father, always conservative in his thinking, later married a religious woman and became more conservative yet. They are not really active participants in D's life. She has four siblings, but her brother, who is in training to be an Orthodox Christian priest, is not close with D. One sister, who is married to a priest, isn't either. She has a good relationship with another sister, and she is close with her mother's family, who have always been accepting of her.

D knits, weaves, sews, makes clothing, and creates sculptures for a living. She is a working artist in her own right. She also works with other artists, providing fabric for their projects. Word of mouth has resulted in lots of freelance opportunities with people who share her love for original art. Since graduating from college D has also worked at various nine-to-fives. At the time of this writing, however, she is unemployed. Most recently, she worked in an art gallery. There is no way to know whether she was let go for economic reasons or because of who she is.

But all in all, she has built a satisfying life for herself. D presents full time and lives her life as a woman. She began seeing a therapist back in high school, when her mom first got sick. Her therapist is not a gender specialist; in fact, she is his first transgender patient. But he knows her well after all these years and has been supportive in helping her to deal with her mother's sickness and death.

D does not feel that being transgender defines her as much as does the loss of her mom. She didn't think of herself as "transgender" until college, when she began to make friends with other people who were transgender and discovered there was a language to talk about how she felt. If anything, being transgender has meant that her understanding of nuance is finer, because it is often useful to be able to grasp subtle overtones when you are trying to prevail in a society that is largely invalidating. Yes, it's true that things are easier for young transgender people today than they were years back, but, as D points out, that is mostly a case of a little looking like a lot by comparison. Other people can take things for granted that she cannot: for instance, filling out a job application that won't conflict with the information on her social security card. Other people can take their privacy for granted. They don't have to worry about a stranger asking them if they are on hormone therapy or if they have had sex reassignment surgery.

D now lives in Oregon and has met a wonderful man who is extremely supportive of her needs. They will be traveling through the country together over the foreseeable future and will eventually settle down in back in Oregon. She reports that life is "really awesome."

Cynthia

Cynthia was born into a strict Catholic family in South Boston and christened Scott fifty-nine years ago as of this writing. She has now changed her name legally, and her sexual reassignment surgery is just a few months behind her. Because she has endured so many other physical challenges over the course of her life, she is still in bed and recovering. Even so, she has no regrets about the surgery, and, in fact, she says it wasn't really all that painful.

Cynthia was the oldest "son" in a six-sibling family. She was the one who was expected to be the "man of the house" when her father was not around. She didn't aspire to manhood. She recognized early on that something was different about her, but she didn't know how to describe it.

The conflict between how she felt on the inside and how she was expected to present herself rendered Cynthia extremely shy throughout her childhood. She could freeze up easily when people spoke to her. Once, when she was about seven, she found an entire box of dresses up in the attic of her house. She hid them and wore them whenever she could. But she had to be very careful, and she had to be quick. Even so, she was conscious of feeling happier and more relaxed when she was able to dress the way she wanted to. She wondered about this other person inside her. She wanted to know more about her, but there was never enough time.

There was no one to talk to about her concerns. Her mother, who probably knew what the problem was even before Cynthia was able to define it, was abusive instead of helpful. She would begin conversations with statements like, "You know, you're supposed to be the son I always wanted." Openings like this made it impossible for Cynthia to talk about what was really on her mind. Her father, a die maker, came home from work cranky after a long day and a two-hour drive and often took his mood out on Cynthia. Even her sisters got into the act, teasing her and hitting her with sticks. If she fought back, she would get punished for hitting girls.

School was no better. Even as a small child she hadn't wanted to go. She missed a lot of school days. She was sick often, but her parents insisted she was faking. Her mother would often chase her out of the house, whacking her with a hairbrush, until she was at the bus stop. Cynthia blacked out on the bus almost every day. When she arrived at school, she was too distracted by her sense of not belonging to pay attention to her studies. It didn't help that she was a puny kid who the bigger kids enjoyed beating on. Girls and boys were divided into separate groups in her school, and when she looked over at the girls from the boys' side of a classroom or in the cafeteria, she would begin to feel peculiar and actually zone out like she did on the bus, and later she would find herself in the nurse's office, where she would learn that her mother had been called and was on her way to pick her up. She told her teachers she was deaf and couldn't hear them. But really she would recoil when people spoke to her, mostly out of fear. Doctors put tubes in her ears, which left scars, but her ability to hear when the peculiar feeling came upon her did not improve. She was held back in the fourth grade, which didn't help her social status.

By the time she was thirteen or fourteen she had figured out that the best way to avoid getting beaten was to hang out with kids who were bad themselves and could offer her brute protection. All she had to do to be part of the group of bad kids was become adept at breaking and entering, as they were. In this way she made a few friends. There were lots of poor people in her neighborhood, lots of people on welfare, and B and Es were fairly common. She was never caught. But even though there was some security in her new relationships, she still remained a loner. There always seemed to be some reminder of her otherness. One day when she was in tenth grade, a kid walked across the lunchroom to where she was sitting and said he recognized Cynthia from years earlier, when they were three or four and he used to come down to Cynthia's yard to play with her and her siblings. "I used to beat the shit out of you," he said. "Don't you remember? I used to break your trucks and beat you up."

Cynthia had been abused so much as a child—by her parents, by her siblings, and by her so-called friends—that the beatings all ran together in her mind as she got older. She had back pain even as a kid, often from being hit by other kids with sticks and shoes, and she would learn from various doctors that she had bulging disks, fractured disks, and other physical ailments. If her father saw her hurting from damage done in the schoolyard or on the way home, he would tell her to be a man and toughen up. "You'll win eventually," he would encourage her.

On her sixteenth birthday she dropped out of school. By then she had to, because in order to continue to hang out with—and thus be protected by—the bad kids, she would have to go further along a path that she was uncomfortable on in the first place. She moved in with her grandmother, who was one of her favorite people. Eventually she did go back to school, but only for a short time because by then she was turning eighteen and her parents told her it was time to get a job.

Cynthia decided to begin a regimen of self-healing. Accordingly, she did what any young man her age would do and got a job as a tool and die maker out in California. It was as macho a job as she could find and not unlike the work her father did. She stayed out west for two years and came home only when she learned that her father, a heavy drinker, was very sick, literally on the verge of drinking himself to death, and her mother needed help in caring for him.

Cynthia found a job on the graveyard shift at a local bakery and took over as much of her mother's responsibilities as possible so that her mother could care for her dad. This included getting the fire going in the woodstove to heat the house in the mornings and making breakfast for the siblings who were still at home before getting them off to school. During the days she attempted to sleep on the sofa, but her mother had a hard time with that. "No one sleeps during the day," she would insist. Sometimes Cynthia would be so tired that she would go out to her car to sleep, or she would find a sunny spot in the woods behind the house. Her father died within year. He was forty-nine.

A few years earlier, before she'd gone out to California, Cynthia had had a girlfriend, but when she tried to explain how she felt about herself, the young woman left. Now she came back again. This time she seemed to understand Cynthia's unconventional tendencies, and she didn't view them as much of an issue anyway since Cynthia was trying to heal herself by going overboard in the other direction and trying to be a good male. Cynthia became a black belt in karate. She left the bakery and returned to tool and die work. The guys she worked with treated her like one of the boys. If anyone bothered her, she would do what guys there did, which was fight with them. "That's the way it works in that world," Cynthia explains. "Someone bothers you, you go out back or into the bathroom and settle it. No one says anything about it afterward. It's over." Having been beaten so many times as a kid, Cynthia was no longer afraid. And now when she was in a fight she usually won. This was the world she was in, so she tried to do what she had to do to be successful in it. But it all caught up with her when she was in her early forties.

She had been married for a while by then, and though she and her wife had drifted apart somewhat, they had three daughters, and they had stayed together. Cynthia and her family were living in a cramped apartment at the time, and her mother was still in the house where Cynthia and her siblings had been raised. Cynthia had always been told that as the oldest son, when her mother was ready to sell the house, it would be offered to her, and for a fair price. It had belonged to her grandfather before it belonged to her parents. The idea was to keep it in the family. But instead of letting Cynthia buy the house, her mom decided to sell it to a stranger. She did this without telling Cynthia, never even giving her a chance to make an offer. Her mother had lied to her, not only on this occasion but all her life. But this was the event that became the straw that broke the camel's back. Everything Cynthia had suppressed for so long came crashing down on her. She was tired of pretending to be what she was not. She was exhausted. Still, it took another six years until Cynthia began to make the transition and started presenting herself in accordance with who she knew she had always been on the inside.

"You Know When You Are Being Truthful."

Cynthia has not told anyone about her recent surgery. Her daughters of course know she dresses, but as one already hates her and another is still on the fence, she didn't want to take the risk of letting them know about this further commitment she has made to be herself. She had the surgery more or less "on the sly," and since she had never been outspoken about her inclinations in the first place, no one has really asked about it. But it has made it difficult for her to seek support. She had one therapist for six years, and he started her on hormones. She also had electrolysis. She didn't require any FFS (facial feminizing surgery) because she passes so well without it. In fact, a few doctors she has seen over the years thought she was a biological woman wanting to change to be a man. All together she has spent between $20,000 and $23,000 to make the transition, none of which has been covered by insurance.

When she was ready to make the transition at work, her therapist refused to call her employer. And her employer refused to call the therapist. Once they knew her intentions, her superiors wouldn't let her back in the die shop. Instead they gave her a desk job in quality control. Cynthia ended up leaving the job as well as the therapist, and while she found another job, for a long time she went without therapy. Only recently has she found a gender therapist and gone on to inform the company where she last worked that she will be presenting as a woman when she returns to the job. But she is not sure she will be able to work again. In addition to a lifetime of back pain that never responded to physical therapy, she now suffers from angina, muscular dystrophy, depression, anxiety, and sleep apnea, and she has had a few strokes.

It may not sound like Cynthia has much to look forward to, but that is not the case at all. If she hadn't made the change and had the surgery, she is certain she wouldn't be alive now. And in spite of everything she is glad to be alive. "You know when you are being truthful," she explains. "You definitely know when what you're doing is the right thing to do." Cynthia is also happy to finally realize that she was not the bad kid her parents painted her to be, that she didn't deserve all the beatings she'd surrendered to all her life.

Cynthia takes things day by day now. The woman she married, whom she refers to as her "sister," continues to be supportive. For last twenty years they have been celibate, but they remain comfortable together to a degree. And they have become accustomed to helping each other financially. She has also renewed a friendship with a woman she was close to years before when she lived in California.

Cynthia's advice for young people suffering from gender identity disorder? "Get help right away. Don't wait. And don't try to heal yourself."

A Poem by Cynthia

Once More

I have stepped my feet once more
Into the valley and the fields
Watch the sun arise again once more
On a long winding tethered pathway
And waiting by the door.

I know you will come for me, my love,
And step into the fields
Watch the sun arise, once more.
From where you shine your light on me
The darkness has been torn and peeled
Like petals off a rose,
Growing out in the field.

No one can ever take from me
Whatever I will feel
My heart, and my love
Will always be out in the fields
On the long and winding tethered pathway
Is still a part of me,
A place I have healed.

Knowing you will come to me, my love
Feel the sun arise again once more
Where you shine your light on me,
The roses in the fields
The long, tethered pathway
A kiss from heaven sealed
As we walked once more
Through the valleys and the fields.

Lauren

"Most Bullying Is Surreptitious."

As of this writing, Lauren is fifty-four years old. Currently she is teaching science (anatomy, physiology, and biology) to high school students.

Her transition at her school took place in 2011, and it went well. Lauren met with the faculty just before summer vacation. Her appearance had already begun to change, so they were not shocked by the news. Lauren had consulted with a friend who had transitioned in a school setting, and she offered some useful pointers. Her friend suggested she not have a separate meeting with parents to discuss her decision. Calling a meeting with parents signals that something is out of order. Parents would surely hear the news from their kids and would then have the option of checking her excellent teaching credentials and drawing their own conclusions.

As for her students, they were mostly great. One young man innocently asked if he would get detention if he accidentally addressed her as "Mr." instead of "Ms." For the first two years after her transition, however, she did come across the occasional miscreant. Once someone spray-painted a penis on the side of the outbuilding where she regularly parked her car. Another time some kids threw marbles into her classroom as they were walking by. She chased them down and was able to identify them (they were caught on camera too), and they were suspended. "Most bullying is surreptitious," Lauren says. "If they were doing this to me, it was incumbent on me to ensure they weren't bullying one another." Of special concern were the LGBT kids.

Lauren is exceptionally sensitive to bullying issues. When she was growing up, her brother was protective and advised her not to act like a "sissy." Outside of the home, she saw the torment another boy, who was called "sissy" and "pantywaist," had to endure. She never wanted to be identified as someone who was vulnerable. Though she knew from the age of five or six that she was different, she also knew how to play the part of someone who fit in. Becoming female was not an option then, so the only recourse was to make sure she learned how to be a guy.

This is not to say that she was able to preside over her environment to her satisfaction. In fact, she considered herself to be a social introvert. She couldn't get the hang of "guy talk." It just didn't make sense to her. She preferred the company of her female friends and her sisters. She preferred the things girls owned to her own possessions. She liked to parade around the house in her mother's high heels. Her brother would tease her, and when she began to cry he would tell her she was "too sensitive." Her friend next door, whose mother was Japanese American, had a collection of porcelain dolls with silk dresses. Lauren found their beauty nothing short of amazing. She wanted a doll; she thought maybe she could get away with a Native American doll that she had seen in one of her mother's S&H Green Stamp catalogs. Her mother compromised and let her pick out a troll doll. But when Christmas came around, Lauren received a cowboy suit, toy gun, and boxing gloves. Was her mother trying to tell her something?

Along with her sister, Lauren had the chance to attend West Point. Her thinking at the time was, *This is definitely going to make a man out of me.* But as she came to see, there were plenty of young women in her classes and various programs who were just as capable as any of the young men. *If a woman can do this*, she began to think, *how can it make me a man?* And she remained incompetent when it came to guy talk.

Still, Lauren was happy with her West Point experience, and she stayed in the military for some time. Though she did not deploy, she was recognized for the being the kind of leader who could be trusted to protect her fellow servicemen and women. She was thought of as having "paternal" qualities, though today she would say this was her maternal instinct in evidence.

Lauren spent thirteen years in the service all told, the last four of which were with the Coast Guard. During that time she performed a number of missions under perilous circumstances, but that did not change the way she felt about herself internally. She felt as though she was always acting, pretending to have a persona that she didn't genuinely experience. She realized that in order to advance in the military, one needed to really "connect" with other officers, including one's superiors, in an informal way. For men, the military is a brotherhood. Although she tried her best to fit in on that level too, she continued to feel frustrated. The other "guys" would tell wild stories and hoot with laughter. They bragged. They cut one another down. Lauren was a chatterbox when she was in her comfort zone, and she had always been articulate. She just couldn't inject the necessary male bravado into her conversations. She felt she was regarded as "straight laced."

Lauren met her first wife, Darla, at a West Point mixer. Although Lauren was socially awkward and shy about sex, Darla was impressed with her, and it was easy for Lauren to be interested in someone who thought so highly of her. She realized even then that Darla had some emotional and psychological problems, but because she was supportive by nature, she didn't see this as much of a problem. She could provide the shoulder Darla would sometimes need to cry on. Also, she was interested in Darla sexually, and that was a good start.

Over time it became clear that Darla was bipolar and suffered from borderline personality disorder. Her depressive episodes would render her abusive and inordinately angry. During her manic episodes she could be fun to be around. Life with Darla was like riding a roller coaster.

The relationship lasted ten years, but at some point during the marriage, Darla decided that she was a lesbian. There had been indications before they'd married, but Darla had tried to cover them up. Darla had her own identity concerns, and she brought up Lauren's cross-dressing during the divorce proceedings to gain an advantage in getting custody of their two daughters.

In order to gain a legal advantage, Darla called the police on numerous occasions, levying false accusations that Lauren had threatened her with physical harm. Darla then filed a restraining order so that she would be awarded primary temporary custody of the children. After many long and dramatic legal episodes, Lauren was vindicated when she was awarded custody of their two daughters in the final divorce decree.

But, it didn't end there. Darla continued to make false accusations that Lauren had violated the year-old restraining order in attempts to regain custody of their daughters. On one occasion, Darla appeared at one of Lauren's clinic appointments and then accused Lauren of stalking her.

Eventually Lauren moved out of state with her fiancée in her attempt to get away from Darla, but she did not have court permission to make the move. Because Lauren violated the divorce decree (parental agreement), Darla was able to regain custody of the girls after three months. A year later she confessed that she was unable to care for them properly, and Lauren got them back again.

Lauren's second marriage to Katy was quite different. Lauren and Katy met on the internet. Not wanting to make the same mistakes over again, Lauren kept a watchful eye out for any sign of psychological disturbances. She didn't observe any. Katy was factual, precise, and decisive. Lauren and Katy married and had a child together, a third daughter for Lauren. For the most part their marriage worked.

Lauren enjoyed caring for the house and taking care of the children. She enjoyed laundry, cooking, preparing school lunches, and other domestic chores, though she had no qualms about yard work and other "macho" tasks either. She would occasionally cross-dress when Katy wasn't around.

The marriage felt like the best of both worlds to Lauren. However, after seven years together, Lauren came to realize that Katy just didn't care about her anymore. In fact, it became increasingly clear that Katy was cheating on her. Once Lauren was certain, she began to explore other aspects of her personality, parts she had kept hidden since childhood.

In 2005, Lauren came down with pneumonia and spent some time at death's doorstep. Katy did not make the time to administer to her, which hurt because Lauren knew that she would have nursed Katy diligently if the situation had been reversed. She realized that her marriage was in serious trouble.

As she regained her health, Lauren had a second and perhaps even more profound realization: she could have died without ever coming to know her real self.

Lauren's near death, combined with the knowledge that her marriage was over, became the catalyst that got her looking for information on the internet. When she was separated from Katy, Lauren joined some groups for men who cross-dressed, but she didn't feel a true affinity with them. It was a different story when she began to meet other transsexuals.

It was as if she had opened a Pandora's box: the more Lauren allowed herself to identify with the women she met, the happier she was and the less she felt she was putting on a front. Her decision to transition came quickly after that, and it felt perfectly natural. What didn't seem natural was that she would have to pretend to be a guy during the work week for some time to come. In the meantime, however, she went forward with counseling and hormones, the combination of which produced significant psychological benefits that helped her feel even more authentic—and alive. Many times she had to ask herself if she would have been able to continue along the path she'd been on if her marriage hadn't broken up. Once she was on her new trajectory, it seemed unimaginable that she hadn't come to it sooner.

Although they were no longer together, Katy seemed to think that Lauren needed her permission to transition. Their daughter was about ten by then, and she overheard Lauren talking about a facial surgery she'd had and another she was anticipating. Breanna was still reeling from the divorce. Now her "father's" appearance was changing too. He was becoming more feminine.

Katy and Lauren's divorce was contentious. During a year-long battle, they agreed to share custody 50 percent of the time. They went back to court. Katy accused Lauren of lying to Breanna, a lie of omission because she hadn't explained her transition to her. Breanna had begun cutting, and Katy insisted this was a reaction to her "father's" behaviors. In fact, both parents knew that Breanna was having issues with boys. Lauren had seen some of the emails she had exchanged with one boy in particular, which spelled it all out. Katy declared that if her cutting had to do with boys, it was only because Breanna was having a difficult time finding masculine role models.

Lauren's custody rights were negated. Now she could see Breanna only every other weekend with a few extra days thrown in here and there. Even worse, the guardian ad litem to whom Lauren would have to appeal was a right-wing religious bigot, not anyone who would understand Lauren's decision to transition. "If you're going to transition, you should do it when your kids are grown up," the ad litem said. "Breanna needs to be the princess." To make matters worse, Lauren's two older daughters not only stopped communicating with her but also testified against her.

Lauren did her homework and had to agree that her daughter was at a tender age for everything that had been thrown at her. But as circumstances couldn't be changed, the second-best option would be support from both parents. Meanwhile, Lauren was reaching the point where her appearance was quite androgynous, which she knew was confusing to people. She didn't feel she could keep up with living in the "in between."

If she waited until Breanna was an adult, Breanna would never know the real Lauren. If Breanna didn't know what was in her heart now, she would likely abandon Lauren when she confronted her as an adult. So many transgender people wait to transition until their kids are grown, only to be rejected anyway. So Lauren did not follow the advice set out by the ad litem.

Lauren was paying child support; and she was running a deficit. If she didn't have certain surgeries within the year, she wouldn't have the money left to have them in the future. She would be stuck in a male body for years to come. She didn't plan to discuss her surgical objectives with Katy, but Katy tapped into her Facebook page and found out about them anyway and reported back to the court. The court authorities were upset. Lauren was upset. In her defiance, she showed up at one court appearance dressed as a woman. She'd already had her new driver's license, which documented her gender identification as female. She had every right to represent herself *as herself*. Nevertheless, the judge persisted in making court orders that referred to her with male pronouns. Lauren was feeling bullied by the court.

The irony here was that Breanna was fine with Lauren's transition. Breanna and Lauren were going to counseling, and there were moments of course when Breanna expressed unease about Lauren's plans, but for the most part, she "got it."

Eventually Lauren found a surgeon who could perform breast, bottom, and brow-lift surgeries all during the same hospital stay, which would be a huge advantage financially. She scheduled her operations for June of 2011. Lauren did not share the details of her surgery with her daughter; however, Breanna learned of the plans while eavesdropping on a phone conversation Lauren had with her mother. Breanna then passed this information on to *her* mother. Lauren was confronted by Katy at the front door when she went to drop off her daughter after the weekend visitation. "How dare you?" Katy asked contemptuously. Lauren noted that it wasn't Katy's decision. She was also concerned that Katy might call the police and levy a false charge in an attempt to thwart her plans for the scheduled surgery. Katy continued her angry confrontation; Breanna placed her hands on her mother's shoulders and turned her away gently. With three simple words—"It's OK, Mom"—Breanna diffused the situation, a gesture that touched Lauren's heart deeply. Before Lauren left, Breanna hugged her. This would be the last time Lauren and her daughter saw each other until after the surgeries.

Postsurgery, Lauren was called back to court and ordered to begin paying an additional $550 a month, not for child support, which she had been paying all along, but to help Katy make her mortgage payments on her condo. Lauren was a teacher. Katy was a school principal. Lauren could only conclude that the judge was punishing her for having gone through with her surgeries. Her finances went from bad to worse.

Nothing is as easy as we would like it to be. Lauren's second daughter from her first marriage still won't communicate with her at this time. Being a participant in a church that mandates a very literal interpretation of the Bible, she is not yet able to comprehend something as complex as a transgender parent. Her older sister is not happy about Lauren's transition but will respond now and then to online messages. However, she has recently mentioned that she too is "getting religion." According to her religious beliefs, it's OK that her mom is a lesbian, as long as she doesn't practice. Being transgender is another story. Lauren is happy to have the full support of her youngest daughter. Recently, she and Breanna and Breanna's boyfriend traveled to Mexico together. Lauren has told Breanna to feel free to call her whatever she wants. Most of the time, Breanna calls Lauren by her first name. Lauren finds it endearing in private moments when her daughter still refers to her as "Dad."

As of this writing, Lauren is at a crossroads in her life. She has been in graduate school for the last year and a half, studying to become a school principal. But she knows when she actually interviews for jobs, she will have to explain an arrest made as a result of false charges during a contentious divorce. The arrest record and male name will follow her to every new job that requires a background check. That means explaining that she is a transgender woman, and while minds and hearts are opening at rates that are unprecedented, there are still plenty of people out there who believe that lesbian, gay, bisexual, and transgender people in school settings are synonymous with child molestation. Nevertheless, Lauren has few regrets about her transition. She says, "When you discover your true self, it is like lifting a shroud of darkness. It would be simply impossible to go backward in time and pretend to be a man again."

A Professional Perspective

People started coming out more and more in the '90s, especially in the Boston area where the International Foundation for Gender Education was headquartered. In fact, after Vernon's store closed down, the IFGE offices moved out of his building and into a building with a lot more space, which they really needed by then. But there would still be (and is still today) a long way for transgender people and cross-dressers to go before they could go about their business without incurring some kind of abuse.

My business has been very successful over the years. I've had to hire other laser hair removal technicians to work with me. I would say about half my clients range from being either occasional cross-dressers to people who are fully in transition from one gender to the other. The transitioning people who come to me are generally the ones who have it together. They are the ones who have been to a physician and/or a therapist and established that they do indeed suffer from gender dysphoria, a conflict between one's physical gender and the gender one identifies as. They are often the ones who have begun to work with a primary care physician and/or an endocrinologist to regulate their hormones.

But that doesn't mean they come bouncing in full of confidence and ready to embrace the future. Some have not told anyone yet what they are doing; some haven't even admitted it to themselves. Even though they are going through the motions, some part of them may be in denial. In fact, even though most come to me with a referral they received from their doctor, there are a few who don't even want *me* to know why their physician recommended hair removal. Others feel very safe in my office; it may be one of the few places where they can experiment a little. Most times they will come into the office in male mode because they have beard stubble, but sometimes a client who still has plenty of facial hair and is only at the beginning of transitioning may come in wearing a dress and a wig, just to try out the new look in a secure environment. Then after the session he may change back into his male clothing and return to work.

Whether they come in with some confidence or without any at all, the people who come to see me are somewhere along in the process and are determined to continue. These people represent approximately 60 percent of the transgender population. The other 40 percent either attempt or succeed in taking their own lives or become victims of hate crimes.

Many of my clients have become my friends over the years. Whether they are straight women who come in to get rid of the hair on their legs so that they never have to shave again or men who are prepping for sex reassignment surgery (also known as gender reassignment surgery), hair removal takes a long time (in some cases), and a lot of relaxed conversation happens in my office during the process. I love talking to people, and I love my job.

From Linda's Office

If you have your brows waxed or plucked or threaded professionally over the course of the years, it may cost you an average of $25 a month, or $300 a year. If you do it from, say, age twenty to age sixty, we are talking 480 visits for a total of $12,000. We are also talking loss of time and waste of energy and the risk of ingrown hairs, possible infections, and irritated or swollen skin. It pays to do your brows permanently. One year of electrolysis, and you're done forever. If you are afraid of having your brows shaped one way and then discovering a shape you like better after time, you can easily start by cleaning up the stray hairs that don't belong on the brow plane and then eventually shape the brows according to your style preference or to coincide with their natural shape. If you do decide to go to an electrologist, be careful of having too much hair removed from the ends of each brow. You may want this as you get older.

Erica

Until recently, Erica presented as a man and was the husband of Cheryl, who died about a year prior to this writing. Erica is the parent of seven children: three from her first marriage (which lasted sixteen years), three stepchildren, and one, her youngest, from her nineteen-year marriage to Cheryl.

Cheryl died of multiple myeloma and plasma cell leukemia. She and Erica battled fiercely to save her life, but in the end, there was nothing either could do. Erica had gone to a therapist on and off for fifty years, and since she needed to talk to someone after losing her beloved Cheryl, she sought out therapy once again. This time, however, she looked for someone who could help her to deal with her grief as well as gender issues she hoped to put behind her for once and for all.

Erica had struggled with gender issues since around the age of six, and possibly even before that. At six, she cross-dressed when she had the opportunity and thought about it when she didn't. She believes now that her parents probably knew but didn't press her about it. She also enjoyed playing with dolls and pretending she was a wife and mother. Playing "house" was a special time for her.

Erica had friends as a kid, but she also got teased for being overweight and not being very athletic. As she got older, she made it a point to become athletic, even though it meant she had to work harder than other "boys" for whom athleticism was natural. But she would still daydream all the time about being a girl. She recalls that she would go to ice-skating shows with her family and would play a game with herself: if the next skater that came out from behind the curtain was female, that would confirm that she would be a female one day. Since most of the skaters were women, she could usually count on getting the result she wanted.

At one point in her early teens, Erica's parents had her go to a therapist, but she didn't know why she was there or what she could say. Out of left field, the therapist said, "Some boys have breasts, you know." She had no idea what he was talking about, and she didn't open up to him then or at any time after. She believed that daydreaming about being a girl was wrong, but she was able to compartmentalize her inclinations on her own and get on with her life. The only real evidence of the burden of her secret was in school. Her fantasies often inhibited her ability to concentrate on what her teachers were saying.

Although the desire to be other than she appeared was with her from a young age, she constantly pushed it aside. It would come back, and she would keep fighting it. Sometimes the impulse was stronger than at other times.

Erica was fortunate to enjoy a happy childhood in spite of her gender identity concerns. She always seemed to be part of organizations, and they offered her distraction. As a kid she belonged to a Jewish youth group where she was well liked and even elected to serve as president.

At the age of eighteen, having graduated from high school, she took a summer job driving an ice cream truck. A local radio station happened to be interviewing kids about their summer jobs, and the company she worked for asked her if she wanted to go on the air to talk about hers. The moment she entered the building where the radio station was located, she knew she was embarking on the path to her future. The host of the show was a kid too. He interviewed Erica about her ice-cream-truck job, and they became good friends. Thereafter, Erica began pitching the executives at the station with her own ideas for shows, and eventually they told her she could come in and do a half-hour pilot. Erica decided to focus on scholastic sports so she could appeal to the station's young audience while also taking the opportunity to demonstrate her own "masculinity" to the public at large. She brought in a tight end from Brockton High, a guy who had just signed to play for Notre Dame, for her first interview.

The executives disliked the show, but they loved Erica. They immediately offered her another show, interviewing kids from "the school of the week." And so began her indoctrination into broadcasting. At the end of the summer she started classes at Boston University, but she still found it difficult to focus. So she switched tracks and enrolled in a broadcasting school, Leland School of Broadcasting, from which she would graduate second in her class.

Erica eventually met with a program director of a radio station owned by a nationally known sportscaster and was hired to do the news, produce a daily two-hour talk show, and fill in as a DJ when needed. She spent over a year at this station, which featured soft rock. She had time, so she also took yet another position with a second station, this one playing big band music.

She was only twenty-one, and her life had already become very exciting. At one of the stations for which she worked, located in Massachusetts but on the border with New Hampshire, she was asked to cover the democratic primaries in New Hampshire. She interviewed several politicians and also Rosalyn Carter, who was campaigning for her husband. George Wallace flew into Warren Airport in Vermont in his private jet to meet with Erica for his interview. He sat in his wheelchair, surrounded by Secret Service, and after the interview he was whisked off again in his plane.

The station manager at one of her jobs drank too much and was abusive. At one point, a quarrel he'd begun with one of the radio announcers became physical. In response, Erica and other staff simply walked out. This meant that sales people and managers had to cover radio shifts. Looking back, Erica sees that this reaction was probably irresponsible, but at the time it seemed like the right thing to do. Thereafter she interviewed for an afternoon news anchor job for a big-league station out of Roanoke, Virginia, but in the end, and because she hadn't yet come to grips with the gender identity issues that were always at the back of her mind, she did not have the courage to accept a job so far away from home. So she took a job with another New Hampshire station, which required her to move to New Hampshire. She had married by then. Even though it was a good position, she didn't want to deal with the commute. So she gave notice and went to work in the family business.

The family business, running a music store, paid well, but it wasn't really a fit for Erica. Her father, who owned the store, had been one of the top trumpet players in Boston. He'd played with many celebrities in his day, including Frank Sinatra, Sammy Davis Jr., Jim Durante, Dean Martin, Louie Armstrong, Nat King Cole, Diana Ross, and others. Erica stayed on for more than a decade and then got into real estate, which would prove to be a good match for her friendly, energetic personality in the years to come. But while she had found her career calling, Erica continued to have misgivings about the gap between who she knew she was and how she presented herself.

By the time Erica was in her late forties, she found herself struggling more than ever with her gender identity. She had planned never to mention it to Cheryl, because she never wanted to upset her. But they boarded a cruise ship to celebrate Erica's forty-ninth birthday, and on the eve of the big day, Erica found herself sharing her concerns with Cheryl. She explained that she often had feminine feelings and that she had cross-dressed in the past. She didn't go into it much more than that. She could tell that Cheryl was having a hard time making sense of her story.

Still, her secret was out, and it did cause some grief and strife between the two. In the end, they were able to continue on with their marriage because they loved each other, and as long as Erica didn't act on her desires, Cheryl wanted to be with her. Every now and then Cheryl would ask Erica a question about her desire to be a woman, and Erica would answer as vaguely as possible so as to avoid confrontation. They had a few arguments here and there about gender issues, but they remained true partners and best friends. They were good to each other. They knew they had something special and could work through any challenges with each other's best interests at heart.

After Cheryl's Passing

Erica spent the last seventeen days of Cheryl's life at her side in the hospital. It was a horrible time, even though they found themselves more fully connected than ever. After Cheryl passed, Erica could not help thinking about how short and fragile life is and how wrong it is to turn one's back on any chance to be happy. She had been happy with Cheryl, and she wanted to find happiness again.

Erica had read about transgender people on the internet. Although she was reluctant to admit that she herself was transgender, she wanted to know more about the transgender community—because she wanted to better understand her own impulses. She told her therapist, well-known gender specialist Diane Ellaborn, that she'd had gender issues all her life but at this point had no idea how she could move forward—or even whether she wanted to move forward. Mostly she just wanted to explore her concerns, because they were persistent. She needed to put them behind her one way or the other.

During her sessions with Diane, much came to light. Erica began to understand that her inclinations were not by choice; it was just who she was. At some point Erica asked Diane for a letter of recommendation so that she could begin hormone therapy. After three months of therapy (the standard time period) and several identification tests that confirmed Erica's suspicions, Diane provided the letter.

Erica made an appointment with an endocrinologist to begin estrogen and testosterone blockers, and in the meantime, during subsequent therapy appointments, she and Diane talked about some of the hurdles she would have to overcome and what reactions she might get from her loved ones when she told them. Diane and Erica agreed that Erica should give her youngest daughter—the only child from her marriage to Cheryl—a good year before dropping the bomb since she was already grieving for the loss of her mother. In the meantime, Erica began laser hair removal and electrolysis.

These were the initial steps in a very long journey. Even so, the hormones made Erica feel more comfortable mentally and physically than she'd ever been before. She had been on blood pressure meds for about twenty years, but once she started hormone therapy, she found she no longer needed them. She wasn't sure if that was because of the hormones themselves—one of which, spironolactone, is known to regulate blood pressure—or because she had less stress in her life now that she no longer had the burden of trying to find a solution for Cheryl's cancer and was slowly but surely giving up the strain of trying to hide her "secret." During one checkup, her blood pressure reading was a perfect 120/70. This is not to say that she wouldn't take back the stress and the high blood pressure in a heartbeat for a chance to be with Cheryl again. Although she already loved being a woman, she would sacrifice that too to be happy with Cheryl. But that was no longer possible. Life goes on, and she had to stay focused on her own happiness. She was making many new friends. For years she'd felt as though she couldn't really share who she truly was, but as her transition advanced, she found she the gap closing. Women began relating to her differently once she began presenting as a woman herself.

She found she was starting to feel differently about men too. It wasn't so much sexual attraction as an awareness that the dynamics of her relationships were changing. She liked men more. She enjoyed looking at them. There was a pool at work (she'd become interested in real estate sales and management over the years), and she noticed that observing men in bathing suits had become a pleasant experience. She could imagine one day exploring what it is like to be a woman with a man.

Once Erica had helped her daughter to settle in at her college in Florida, she began to live as a woman full time, except at work or when she was with the other children. In the beginning she couldn't tell what people were perceiving. Did she pass? She didn't feel she was being gawked at, anyway. When she traveled to the western part of state for treatments and stayed at a hotel, men opened doors for her, and people treated her with the kind of consideration that is usually reserved for the fairer sex. Other women were especially nice to her. They approached her in the breakfast lounge at her hotel and just start chatting. People didn't seem to think of her as biological male.

By this time Erica had already talked to her two oldest daughters, her sister, and a few friends. She was hoping that when the time came, the older adult children would be able to offer support to her youngest daughter. She visited Julie, her middle daughter (from her first marriage), in Pennsylvania and told her while they were out at a restaurant. Julie didn't say much there, but when they got back to the house she became very emotional. She took her cell phone out into the yard and called Erica's sister, who already knew. Thereafter Julie began to investigate transgender issues on the internet. Once she started to get information and build a network for herself wherein she could communicate with other adult children of transgender individuals, she began to get comfortable with the idea. She agreed that Erica deserved to be happy.

Before leaving Pennsylvania that day, Erica had asked Julie to keep Erica's disclosure to herself. But Julie asked for permission to tell her husband, Sean, who was a marine recruiter. When he learned, he called to speak to Erica. Erica was afraid to hear what he would say. To her great joy, he said, "Papa, we love you very much. You deserve to be happy. Our family totally supports you." Julie also asked Erica to inform her older sister, Kim, so that she would have someone to discuss the situation with. Kim broke down and cried when she found out, but she hugged Erica and told her she loved her and would support her decision in any way she could. Kim asked Erica to tell her husband, Steve. Although surprised, Steve offered full support and told Erica he loved her. And so it went.

Erica came out thereafter to her wife's closest friend, a woman who was very progressive in her thinking and very supportive. She invited Erica to come for dinner dressed as her true self. Erica found that they were able to connect that evening on a level they had never attained before. Their relationship evolved into a close friendship.

Shortly thereafter, Erica attended her first First Event conference and was happy to realize that she felt very much like the confident woman she'd always wanted to be. She and Cheryl used to tease their daughter that she could make friends anywhere, at any time. At First Event, Erica experienced that ability herself.

Finally the time came for Erica to tell her youngest daughter, Jackie. At first Jackie flipped out. "I lost my mom, and now my father is becoming a woman! I can't believe this is happening," she cried. But she was miserable only for a day and a half. Then she went to Erica and said, "Dad, I love you. It doesn't matter to me if you're a man or a woman. Can I have a new car?" (The answer to her question was yes.)

Once everyone knew, Erica's daughter Julie decided all the females in the family should take Erica out for a "girl's only" night. Sitting there at dinner, surrounded by her loved ones—or at least the females among them—laughing and having a good time, Erica couldn't believe that this had become her life. Two of her three step-children had trouble wrapping their heads around her transition, but even they declared their love. And while they did not promise support, it would eventually come.

When Erica first told her kids, she imagined she would have fully transitioned by October 2014. Her daughter Ashley was getting married over Labor Day 2014; Erica planned to attend the wedding not as Erica but as Rick so as not to upset the applecart. But as it happened, she transitioned in July. To her delight, Ashley told her to come as Erica. She was overwhelmed. She bought a dress. One of her sons-in-law walked her down the aisle.

Her younger daughter, Jackie, had Parents' Weekend at her college in September, again at a date that turned out to be after Erica's transition. By then Jackie was a sophomore at Florida Atlantic University. Jackie also said she was good with Erica attending as herself—but she had one caveat: Jackie's boyfriend Phil knew about Erica's transition, but his brother Lenny, with whom Jackie had had some issues, did not. Jackie was afraid that if Lenny found out, he would ridicule her. Therefore, Jackie asked Erica to attend the Parents' Weekend football game, where she would meet Phil and Lenny's father, as Rick. Erica was glad to go to the football game as Rick if that was what her daughter felt was needed.

However, the night before the football game, Phil's father surprised Erica by calling to invite her for dinner. The event that followed was as tense and tender as any scene from *La Cage aux Folles*. Phil's mom had been told about Erica's transition and was dying to get Erica alone to ask her questions. Phil's dad had met "Rick" the year before and couldn't get over how different he looked. Later he asked Phil if everything was OK with Rick. Phil assured him things were fine. The group attended the football game together the next day and everything was good, but when Phil's dad invited Rick out for another dinner, Erica had to decline. She just couldn't do it again. Also, she'd only brought along one set of male clothes. Once she got off the phone with Phil's dad, she took those clothes and dumped them in the trash can in the lobby.

Erica prepared for facial surgery to advance her hairline and give her forehead and chin a more feminine contour. She changed all her documents to her new name and let just about everyone know about her transition, including the woman who works in the store where she stops to get a bagel in the morning. Some might wonder why she would bother to tell a near stranger, but Erica refused to play make believe. Her acquaintances have responded to her honesty. One day, the woman at the bagel store stopped her. "I have something to tell you," she said. *Uh-oh*, Erica thought, and she waited for the other shoe to drop. The woman continued: "You are absolutely beautiful." That made Erica's day.

After she came out, Erica received many text messages from friends and family expressing how they were inspired by her authenticity. Here are some of the best:

From a fifty-year-old nephew on her wife's side: "I wanted to tell you how your courage and determination has blown me away and that you're my new hero."

From her daughter Jackie's friend, to Jackie: ". . . thank you for allowing me into your life tonight and letting me meet SUCH an incredible woman. I know I speak for LeAnne, Nicole and I when I say we had SO much fun tonight, and we honestly wouldn't have rather been anywhere else in the world . . . You have a truly incredible dad who cares more about you more than anything in the world, and I can see that you are EVERYTHING in her eyes. It honestly meant the world to me that you would let me come tonight and let me meet such an incredible person who is just BEAMING happiness . . . I seriously hope that one day I'm as happy and confident with myself as she is."

Text from her sister-in-law's friend: "I loved the closet tour!!! I am so happy for you. I wish you all the best. The real you is wonderful!!! I'm sorry you had to not be yourself for so long, but now is your time, and it is all good."

Text from coworker: "I was thinking of you, and it made me smile."

Erica's surgeries have all been successful. She is working now as a successful executive for a Greater Boston real estate firm, has begun dating men, and is living happily. "Everything is awesome," she reports.

Nicki
How You Go to Your Grave Matters

Nicki grew up "Dominic" in a tough Italian Catholic neighborhood on Long Island.

She was the middle boy in the family. Both her younger and older brothers were tall, big-boned, powerful boys who commanded respect even in that macho environment. Though Nicki had not inherited the same genes for height and breadth, she was safe from physical abuse when they were around. When they weren't, it was another story. She got the crap beaten out of her regularly.

Even though she avoided fighting as much as possible, there was still pressure on her to be "a guy," to behave the way other boys behaved. She put on the act and did her best, but in truth she had no real interest, and her best was never quite good enough anyway. She enjoyed being with her mom. She liked to bake and help around the house. She liked sitting and chatting with female cousins and their friends. She especially liked hanging out with her older sister when she was getting ready for dates. Talk was so easy with her. Nicki didn't know why. She liked fashion, but she knew better than to say so.

She didn't fit in, and she wasn't a happy kid. In spite of the large number of siblings and cousins in her family, she felt isolated. In her effort to fill the void, she turned to reading, writing, and church. Reading offered genuine if temporary escape. The church offered opportunities to volunteer in outreach programs, including working with the disabled and the elderly. Nicki loved doing this kind of work. She learned early on that in spite of the fact that she had few friends, she had a great capacity for compassion, especially for those who were somewhat marginalized.

She wasn't sure if she was gay or straight. She wanted to talk about her feelings and her confusion, but she was a guy, and guys didn't talk about things of that nature. And it only would have led to trouble anyway, given her family credo. One of her cousins had beaten up a gay guy in a train station, and he had become something of a hero within the clan as a result. Another particularly violent cousin became a war hero. The men in her family—her father, her male cousins, her uncles—believed that any kind of gender variation was intolerable. Theirs was a culture of violence. Nicki's father thought nothing of whacking his sons when they disappointed him. Her brothers could take it. They would get hit and talk back and get hit some more, and when it was all over they didn't think twice about it. For Nicki it didn't go away. She knew her father loved her, but she could not get over the trauma of having him beat her. In this environment, there was no way she could express her aversion to her own maleness.

In order to survive, Nicki learned to compartmentalize her emotions. The low-level depression that resulted was at least manageable. She cross-dressed a few times when she was twelve or thirteen, but she was able to tell herself that it was just some sort of sexual release. It felt good to be in girl's clothing. In fact, it felt so right that on one occasion she was too slow to change back into her boy garb, and her mom caught her, and her dad found out. For the first time Nicki could remember, her father was speechless. He didn't even beat her. Her parents threatened to take her to a psychiatrist. But they were too embarrassed and ashamed to actually follow through.

For Nicki, it wasn't just about the clothes anyway. It was something more than that. If someone had said to her back then, "You're not gay; you just want to be a woman; in fact, you are a woman on the inside," it all would have made sense. But of course no one said that. Accordingly, her confusion continued, and always it led to dead end, a place where common language was inadequate to provide the answers she needed.

After high school, Nicki left New York to attend college in Maine. She had hoped to leave the past behind as well, but it followed her. Sometimes she was depressed; sometimes she felt suicidal. The college in Maine, she soon learned, was another macho environment. She dated women, but it was less out of lust than out of a desire to know what it was like to *be* them. She admired their beauty. She thought about what it would be like to have a body like that, a face like that. She knew other guys didn't feel this way. She wanted someone to hold her and kiss her the way she knew the women she found herself with wanted to be held and kissed. But she wasn't particularly interested in gay men either. She went from one relationship to another. When she had sex with a woman, she tried to flip the coin and imagine that someone was penetrating her rather than the other way around.

Nicki got married, and soon after her wife (now her ex-wife) got pregnant. Her son was born. She knew getting married had been a mistake, but she didn't know what the right path for her even looked like. Her daughter came along next. By now Nicki, who had gotten her degree in psychology, was working as a special education teacher. She loved her job; she loved her children; it should have all worked, but it didn't.

She and her ex-wife stayed together for fifteen years. They had never been compatible on any level, but they held it together for the sake of the kids. Their divorce was exceedingly painful. In her effort to deny Nicki visitation rights, Nicki's ex-wife told her lawyers about Nicki's identity confusion and painted her as being mentally ill. This resulted in Nicki being fired from her job and losing her equity in the house. As for her children, her visits had to be supervised. Nicki fought back, spending money designated for her retirement to ensure that she could spend time with her kids. During the course of the marriage, Nicki had converted to Judaism to please her ex-wife. Now the rabbi, who had been Nicki's friend, turned on her along with everyone else and wanted to testify against her. The only ray of light in that dark time was a therapist by the name of Alice Bloom. Nicki and her ex had gone to Alice together to find a way to make their divorce more amicable. After a few meetings, Alice suggested Nicki's ex see someone else and that Nicki come to see her alone. In subsequent meetings Alice voiced what Nicki had in all these years never actually admitted to herself: Nicki responded to life more as a woman than as a man. And furthermore, that didn't make her a bad person. It was as if someone had discovered Nicki's darkest, most deeply hidden secret and brought it to the surface where even Nicki could see it clearly. "Am I right?" Alice asked. Nicki knew she was. Nicki had found a place, finally, where it was safe to verbalize her feelings, and she let them pour out. It was a tremendous relief. Nicki worked with Alice for about a year, but because she had lost her job, she had no choice but to seek work in a community where she could start over. She moved from Maine to Massachusetts.

Alice had encouraged Nicki to join the Tiffany Club once she settled in her new state, but Nicki was afraid. She had grown up surrounded by people who associated any kind of sexual or gender deviation with porn, racy magazines, and a world that was twisted and totally X-rated. Now that she had brought her secret to the surface, she wanted to bury it again and go on with her life. Over the years she had learned to be funny, jovial, to talk about sports. She intended to go to her grave as she was, a man—albeit a man with a secret. Nobody, not even Alice, had told her that her efforts would be in vain.

Nicki got a job working as the director of the special education department in a high school. She was depressed but functioning. She had perfected her childhood knack for pigeonholing those issues she didn't want to think about, and she now put that skill to good use. She had two relationships with gay men, but both broke up with her when they realized she herself was not a gay man. She had always been well read. Now she read more: Dante, Chaucer, the Bible. She wasn't experiencing the joy she suspected was out there, but at least she had learned from Alice that she was not a bad person. Alice had opened that door.

Nicki says her second wife had every reason to be angry at her. Even though Nicki was dressed when they met, Nicki led her to believe that she could shake off her inclinations and make their relationship work. But the effort cost her. She gained over 100 pounds and was well on her way to a heart attack. She was eating her way to an early death. Luckily, the school where she worked sponsored a weight-loss contest, and Nicki actually won, losing 110 pounds over a period of six or seven months.

By the time Nicki turned forty-nine, she and her second wife had been together for thirteen years. Nicki excelled at work; she had a fine house to replace the one she lost back in Maine; and she had solid, loving relationships with both her children. She had tried very hard to keep the promises she had made to herself and to her loved ones. But something was still wrong. It had been wrong for years and years, and suddenly she realized that it had only been building all this time. There was no way she could go to her grave in a man's body after all.

From Linda's Office

Nicki, who had a mix of black and gray hair on her face and body, came to me in 2013 at age fifty. She wanted an aggressive program to remove her beard. We used a combination of electrolysis and laser treatments to clear her unwanted hair, beginning first with laser and introducing electrolysis later.

Nicki's treatments were completed in about fourteen months. By then she'd had forty sessions, including twenty-five hours of laser treatments (for a total of $2,000) and forty-three hours of electrolysis (for a total of $3,800). The electrolysis was necessary to remove the gray hairs because the laser doesn't recognize gray or light-colored roots. Had she not been a candidate to use the laser first to eliminate the darker hairs in her beard, removal of her beard could have taken about two hundred hours. Because we were able to use the laser, she saved about $14,000. (Note: Removing a beard solely with electrolysis can take between one hundred to four hundred hours, and in some instances even longer.)

Nicki traveled one and a half hours one way (three hours round trip) for her weekly sessions. She used a numbing cream on her skin when she had to have electrolysis so that she wouldn't feel any discomfort or pain. With her vigorous work schedule and the long drive required to reach our office, she was relaxed and sometimes even able to sleep during her sessions. She found them to be very therapeutic. And it made her happy to know with each session she was a little bit closer to becoming her real self. None of her black hairs have come back; her skin remains smooth and perfectly clear!

I consider Nicki one of my best cases in that we cleared her beard in record time for someone in her age group. Younger people, who don't have any gray and can therefore undergo more laser treatments, can usually expect to spend less time and money than older people.

Just the Beginning

That acknowledgment has brought her more joy and peace than she ever expected to experience. She's fifty-one now and terrified about the journey ahead. Anything can go wrong at any time. She still has her job, and while her boss and the admin staff know about the path she is on, Nicki acknowledges that she can be fired at any time, ostensibly for any number of considerations. In the state of Massachusetts there are no other transgender people working in education that I know of. All she can do is wait and hope it will all turn out well. As for her children, they say they still love her, but she doesn't know if they will really be able to accept her once her transition is complete. And while her wife is still with her, Nicki admits that their marriage sometimes feels like a ride on a roller coaster. Nicki has watched her brave and wonderful spouse go through a range of emotions over the last few years. She understands, but that doesn't necessarily make it any easier.

Nicki doesn't want to lose everything all over again, but she will if she has to. She doesn't have a choice anymore. She has received her diagnosis from the famous gender therapist Diane Ellaborn. She's been on hormones now for almost six months. She doesn't know where she is going to get the money for facial and sex reassignment surgeries, but that's next on the list. She has joined support groups now and learned that there is great dignity in being who you really are. She respects herself. For the first time in her life she is able to say, "This is me. Here I am."

"Angels of Diversity," from Nicki's Blog Site

It was to be a busy day. I had already had a wig consultation, and later I would be going with my wife to a dinner party many miles from our house. When you are transgender, you often travel great distances to be in the presence of like-minded souls. It was my desire to get my nails done before going out so that I might effect a better, more natural presentation.

I decided to visit a salon I had been to many times before. Generally this salon is not that crowded on weekends. It has always been easy for me to "walk in" and get an appointment more or less immediately. So I was surprised when I opened the door to find the place packed, with every technician busy with customers. To make matters worse, there were seven or eight teenage girls in the waiting area. My newfound feeling of taking on the world, brought on by the success of the wig consult, vanished. Girls can be so brutally honest. And they often lack restraint. I wanted to leave, but some crazy, stubborn sensibility told me not to go anywhere. I had come to get my nails done, after all.

I sat down among the girls, who ranged in age from twelve to seventeen. For a fifty-one-year-old trans woman who is still working on such basics as walk, voice, mannerisms, and overall presentation, you could not find a more daunting set of potential judges. But whether I would become the object of everyone's derision or not, I was not going to back down.

I busied myself on my iPhone. Though I had forgotten my glasses and could not see a single text message, I proceeded to type blindly to a few friends to try and describe the situation I was in at that moment. In doing so, I could see the humor in my circumstances. Two friends texted back to me, but I couldn't read what they wrote. Still, I felt supported and somewhat calmer.

There were girls all around me, but I found myself most aware of the two girls sitting on a couch directly in front of me. A woman, their mom, was standing nearby. She had a kind face, and she smiled frequently as she watched her children interacting, exclaiming over the magazine they were looking at together. I gave up on the phone and began to page through a magazine myself. Dear God, *I thought,* this could be it. I could get teased and harassed by girls younger than my own daughter, and I would be completely defenseless. *I reminded myself of the narcissism of adolescence. Girls this age were usually too absorbed in the question of who might be taking them to the prom to want to harass a transsexual trying to find her way in the world.*

I glanced up. The girls were still looking at the magazine. The mother was still smiling admiringly. No one was looking at me. I returned back to my magazine, but I stiffened when I heard the younger girl begin to giggle. I dared to glance up again. The older girl was pointing to a photo in her US magazine. The younger girl was saying that she wanted to kiss whoever it was in the picture. Girls can be so silly. The older girl was laughing too now. She commented that her sister wanted to kiss everyone in the magazine.

I dared to take another look, and this time I noticed what I hadn't noticed previously: the younger girl had Down syndrome.

Her smile and laughter were contagious, and soon everyone in the reception area and even in the salon beyond was smiling in her direction. It was clear that everyone was feeling blessed to be in her company. The sisters bantered back and forth and the mother went on enjoying them. When they were done laughing about all the people in the magazine whom the younger sister wanted to kiss, the girls took selfies with the older one's smart phone. By then I had figured out that they were waiting for yet a third sister, who was getting her nails done. I was no longer self-conscious. I smiled at their antics like everyone else. I was a human being among other human beings. This lovely girl, so happy in her world, unencumbered by some of the more unpleasant facts of diversity, was transmitting a message of love.

For the twenty or so minutes the woman and her daughters were there, that salon housed an older transgender woman and a sweet young woman with Down syndrome. The world had room for the both of us.

People can and will show kindness to those they deem beneath them, but sometimes in the act of opening their hearts to one individual, their gift of understanding increases generally. As all the technicians and customers made room in their hearts and minds for this young woman, I slipped on in through the door too. That young woman's innocence reminded the people around her that we are all part of one family. She offered each of us the opportunity to be better human beings. Her laughter shattered prejudice. To me she gave the strength I needed to pick my head up and embrace my life, in that moment at least.

From Linda's Office

Sophie came in at age sixteen. She had been on blockers since puberty. Her blockers (and estrogen product) came to her via an implant in her arm. Her work totaled about seven hours (420 minutes) and consisted primarily of the removal of vellus hair (otherwise known as peach fuzz). Many biological females have peach fuzz on their faces and never give it a second thought, but Sophie, who suffered OCD, did not want to feel any hair at all on her face.

Sophie did not have SRS prep work done because the doctor with whom she'd scheduled her surgery preferred to clean out hair follicles himself during the process. To the best of my knowledge, *most* SRS doctors currently working in the United States require hair removal in preparation for SRS. However, some doctors outside the country (for instance, some in Canada and Thailand) do not want hair removed.

Katie

A Fairy-Tale Transition

Katie was so young when she knew that she can't even remember that far back. She just always remembers knowing. When she was two or three she told her mother that she was her daughter not her son. Her parents were concerned but not angry. They lived in San Francisco at the time, and her mom was easily able to find an LGBT bookstore where she could search for more information. While she was there going through the racks, she happened to meet a transgender woman, and they wound up talking about Katie. The woman said that the law stipulated that you had to be over eighteen to have sex reassignment surgery but that Katie's parents would be wise to let her dress as she wanted in the meantime. Thereafter her parents let her wear dresses in the house, but in public she continued to present as a boy.

When Katie was four, the family moved to Connecticut and Katie started school as a boy. She recalls that she dressed that first year as Dorothy from *The Wizard of Oz* on Halloween, and that was a relief for her. But the day after she went back to presenting as a boy. She was confused, and her confusion made her feel somewhat isolated, but she had a lot of friends, male and female, and while she didn't care for sports, her male friends were mostly intellectual introverts who didn't care for them either.

When she was ten Katie watched an episode of *Ugly Betty* in which a character previously referred to as Alex Meade comes out as Alexis Meade, a transgender woman. Katie knew at that moment that the inner turmoil Alexis professed to have felt as Alex was

189

exactly the same as the confusion she had experienced all her life. She was very happy to know there was a solution. But she was under the impression that gender transition surgery was for the very rich only, and she didn't expect to be that wealthy for some years to come. She figured by the time she was thirty she would be able to follow Alexis's example.

Then when she was thirteen, she saw another TV show, *Law & Order: Special Victims Unit*, in which a man is beaten for his lack of support regarding his teenaged transgender daughter's desire for gender reassignment surgery. In this episode the teen is eventually able to go on puberty blockers as a prelude to transitioning.

That was all the encouragement Katie, who was just starting puberty, needed. She came out not long after to a family friend, who helped her come out to her parents. Her parents were not very surprised, and that was when they told Katie how she'd insisted that she was their daughter and not their son when she was just a toddler. They were also able to list a lot of other indicators they had noticed over the years. After coming out to her parents, Katie told her younger sister and then her teachers and her friends at school. Everyone was supportive. Katie's mom helped her to find a therapist and also an endocrinologist who started her on both puberty blockers and then hormones.

Katie had taken advanced classes and even extra classes over the years, so she was about to graduate a year early from high school. She knew the life she wanted, and now she was in a hurry to move on with it. She began taking classes at a local community college and also took on a job in a computer store. She had her surgery in May 2014 at the age of eighteen.

Her surgical experience was nearly as effortless as her coming out had been. It went well, and she was back on her feet in a week. That's not to say that there weren't challenges in the months leading up to the surgery. She'd been putting on an act for years, pretending to be someone she was not. The closer she got to transitioning, the more she felt like a blank slate, and she was anxious about how she would eventually fill it. Her only bona fide regret is that she didn't do it sooner. When she thinks back on her childhood she sees a lot of years wasted because she had to experience them as a boy.

Katie doesn't think of herself as a transgender young woman. She's just a young woman, like any other . . . if you don't consider her past. Being female feels absolutely normal to her.

As of this writing, Katie continues to live with her parents and her younger sister, all of whom have been great about her transition. In fact, her mother has become the president of the local LGBT center and an advocate for LGBT issues generally. Katie has decided to take next year off from college and work full time. Like many other savvy computer geeks, she will be working in an Apple Store. She didn't really date before her transition, and she's not really dating now. She was in a rush to make her transition, because she had no doubts whatsoever, but she's not in a rush to fill up her "blank slate": she's taking her future one day at a time.

While she is not running out to become a media darling, she did agree to do one TV show in Australia, because she does want to let other young people like herself know that they are not alone. She may do more TV in the future. She doesn't want to ever be exploited.

Remembrance

As previously mentioned, most of the people who come to see me are well on their way to "becoming" who they really are. This book is about them, written both to support the efforts of those who will eventually follow in their footsteps and to educate people who want to learn more about who transgender people are and what they go through in order to simply be themselves. As of this writing, there are about 1.4 million transgender people living in the United States. That's 0.6 percent of the population. Approximately 12 percent have gender reassignment surgery. And while this book focuses on the unique profiles of twenty of them, I think it's important to remind readers again that some 40 percent of transgender people will never find themselves in a book like this, sharing their success stories, because they don't get that far. They are the ones who commit suicide. Or they live out their lives and go to their death beds with their missed opportunity to transition as the biggest regret of their lives.

Forty percent of 1.4 million is an incredibly high number. It is significantly greater than the number of vets who try or succeed in taking their lives, and perhaps more than twice the percentage of lesbians, gays, and bisexuals who do so. According to recent research, the percentage of suicides and suicide attempts within the general population is less than 5 percent.

Most of the transgender people who attempt and/or succeed at suicide are people who made efforts to "come out" or who did not intend to reveal their secret but were found out anyway. As a result of either coming out or being found out these people experienced rejection, harassment, discrimination, and/or violence. Obviously, there is a very clear connection between abuse and suicide. If we were, individually and as a society, to embrace rather than reject people we consider to be different than us, the suicide rates would decrease very quickly.

It sounds so easy, doesn't it?

One suicide story that has stuck with me over the years is the story of Roxy. Roxy's suicide was totally avoidable. Roxy *did* come out, to a gorgeous Swedish woman whom she met at a gay bar. Though the Swedish woman was straight, she liked to be with a diverse crowd, she said, and Roxy, who was still presenting as a man at the time, felt safe sharing "his" secret with her.

They started dating and fell in love. The Swedish woman said at first that she loved Roxy for having both a male and a female nature; she was in love with both parts of Roxy. Roxy felt empowered enough to begin dressing as a woman, then, in fact, become Roxy. But while Roxy's Swedish lover put up with it, over time she let Roxy know that she intended to change Roxy back into a man. She was into some kind of witchcraft, and she insisted that she would put spells on Roxy until Roxy no longer felt transgender at all. Roxy wanted to take the transition all the way, to have sex reassignment surgery and any necessary facial surgery, but the Swedish lover insisted that would never happen; it wouldn't be necessary once the spells began to take effect. With no way out, Roxy hung him/herself in the basement.

Another Story from the Other 40 Percent

Recently, while I was visiting my sister in her hair salon, I picked up a copy of the local paper and read in the obits about a woman, a girl, who died at the age of fifteen. Let's call her Z. The most prominent features in the accompanying photo of Z were her partially shaved head and her extremely sad, almost pleading expression. Also, she looked a lot more like a boy than a girl.

During the drive home I found myself overwhelmed with concern for her. The obit text said that she loved art, music, drama, and *Star Trek*. I kept thinking of the future a creative kid like Z could have had. I told my husband about Z, and we looked her up on the internet and learned that she had vague connections to a few transgender organizations. One, in its expression of sympathy for Z, had written "It's too bad this happens so many times" in a comment box on the obit site.

The drug that killed Z, we learned, is called 25I-nbome, or N-Bomb. It's a psychedelic like LSD, and it looks like and is administered in the same way as LSD. But LSD has been around for a number of years, and there is disagreement among researchers about whether or not it can kill people directly. N-Bomb *is* a killer. It produces confusion, difficulty communicating, paranoia, seizures, and, often, death. Those who don't die often experience kidney problems.

I had to ask myself why someone like Z, who appeared to have everything to live for, would take a drug like N-Bomb, and I kept coming back to the same conclusion. She suffered from gender dysphoria. She had made some half-hearted attempts to reach out to organizations that might have helped her, but she didn't hit on any lifesaving results.

Recently, while I was doing electrolysis on a transgender person who had been in previously for laser work on her beard, I told her the story of Z, and then I opened up and told her about my sister Jodi, who put a gun to her head at age seventeen, in 1986. She responded, "Do you want to hear something eerie? My brother at twenty years old put a gun to his head." I asked her if he had been TG (transgender) too. She said he was, but the family didn't know; her brother didn't understand what was happening in his body either.

After that story, I went on a mission to donate my services to at least a few young people who might not otherwise reach out to me. I met two teens at First Event, a conference for transitioning people at which I am a regular vendor. These teens were standing alone, with their heads down, appearing to be shy. I offered my services to them pro bono. They almost didn't believe it was real. Another woman (who acts as a Big Sister for transgender people) and I are working together to help these two individuals achieve their goals. She donates her time, picking them up in locations far apart, bringing them to my office for their facial hair removal treatments, and treating them to lunch on the drive home. They are already happier young people. If we can make their world a better place, that makes us happier too.

Transgender Day of Remembrance

November 20 is a special day set aside to commemorate people who have died or been killed as a result of transphobia—the hatred or fear of transgender and gender nonconforming people. It was started by one trans woman back in the late '90s and since then has evolved into an international day of action that can include candlelight vigils, parades, art and music, dancing and other performance shows, interviews, etc. On the one hand we seem to be heading in the direction of tolerance; on the other, it could be a long time until we get there.

From Linda's Office

The trans women who come to see me have often spent years trying to rid themselves of facial hair on their own, by shaving, plucking, tweezing, or waxing. Some also began electrolysis elsewhere and came to me after a move, a break, or an unsuccessful experience elsewhere. My role as their technician depends not only on their age, genetics, hair color, skin color, and the medications (including but not limited to hormones) they take but also on their own efforts to rid themselves of unwanted hair previously as well as the level of skill and experience of any technician / professional hair removal practitioner who may have worked on them in the past.

Holly
A Life of Service

Holly Ryan is a parent, a homeowner, a supervisor, a state committee member for the Democratic party, a sports fan, a good cook, and a transsexual woman.

In 2012 she was appointed by the mayor of Newton, Massachusetts, to serve a three-year term on Newton's Human Rights Commission. The commission, which was established in 1973, works to ensure that everyone—regardless of race, sex, color, sexual orientation, age, disability, national origin, or ancestry—has equal access to employment, housing, education, and public accommodations. There are very few transgender people nationwide in leadership positions with city, state, or government agencies. Holly's appointment will likely open the door for many others in the future.

The executive director of MassEquality acknowledged that the appointment was "a huge step for the transgender community" and it "shows that society is changing and because of that, we all benefit when citizens like Ms. Ryan are given the opportunity to participate in her community this way."

As part of the conversation as well as the community, Holly was able to help forge and testify on behalf of the Transgender Equal Rights Bill, which was signed by Governor Deval Patrick on November 23, 2011. As of the signing, Massachusetts became the sixteenth state to officially offer protections against discrimination to transgender people in housing, credit, employment, and public education. According to the Associated Press, there are estimated to be thirty-three thousand transgender citizens living in Massachusetts.

Prior to her Human Rights Commission appointment, Holly served as the director of Purchasing and Foodservice for the Middlesex Human Service Agency, a nonprofit, multiservice organization that cares for the homeless and helps those with substance abuse problems. She has also served as a consultant for the transgender community in Boston—including as Chair of the Massachusetts Transgender Political Coalition, a member of the Massachusetts Department of Public Health's Bureau of Substance Abuse Services LGBTQ Advisory Board, a board member of Bay State Stonewall Democrats, and an elected member of the Massachusetts Democratic State Committee.

As of this writing, it has been twenty-three years since Holly made her transition back in a time when there were no employment protections for transgender people in Massachusetts. She received full support from the CEO of her company at that time. That meant that what anyone else thought about her decision wouldn't hold any weight, at least not in the workplace.

At the time of her transition, Holly was raising two children. She was paying half their insurance, buying their equipment for their music and sports pursuits, etc. If she hadn't received her supervisor's support, everyone in her life would have suffered, particularly her children. They would not have been able to continue in the same schools or wear the same clothes or even live in the same house. Holly stresses how important it is for outsiders to understand that the rejection of a transgender person can be rejection of an entire family.

Holly knew the move was the right one for her, that making the transition would allow her to live what has turned out to be an extremely worthwhile life of service to others. She had known since she was seven years old that she was meant to be a woman, but she didn't officially transition until she was forty-five. She does not talk about the physical aspects of her transition in interviews.

Transitioning one's gender is a process that includes changing one's clothes and hairstyle, as well as the pronoun used to describe oneself and possibly one's first name. It can also include hormone replacement therapy and sex reassignment surgery—but it may not. There are plenty of transgender people who cannot afford to have sex reassignment surgery—or who choose not to. The surgery does not make the difference and should therefore not be part of the criteria for defining a transgender person.

Holly had two goals in life: she wanted to raise a family, and she wanted to have a great job. As she points out, "All trans people want is to have the same thing others have, to be able contribute to their communities and cities and to be free of discrimination." Holly wanted to be able to live a wonderful life like everyone else, and she can truly say that has come to pass.

Ashlee

An Outsider Makes Her Way In

Ashlee grew up in a small rural community in upstate New York. Back in the '80s this was not a region where a young person could easily voice concerns about her gender identity. Although she was a male biologically, ever since her preteen years Ashlee had suspected she had a strong feminine side. The older she got, the more this became a certainty. This awareness made it difficult for her to feel comfortable and make friends in her small, provincial high school.

But gender identity was not the only thing that made her feel like an outsider; Ashlee didn't *look* like anyone else either. She was Asian in all-white setting. Her Polish father and English/Dutch mother had adopted her from Korea when she was a toddler. The combination of a Celtic first name, a Polish last name, and Asian looks made her an enigma in her town, especially in her high school. Some kids made fun of her. She had a few friends, but she was quiet and shy and dared not express her feelings. She didn't like typical male activities, but she engaged in them to the extent that she appeared to conform. Not surprisingly, she felt very alone growing up.

Ironically, one of Ashlee's siblings, who was also adopted—though not from a foreign country—suffered a gender identity crisis too. Had both Ashlee and Stephanie known what the other was going through, perhaps they could have helped each other. But they went through their journeys separately in those days. Stephanie was a year and a half older. She had different friends; she responded to her identity concerns in a different manner—including an early entry into the world of drugs. Ashlee and her sister didn't get along; there would be no communication between them for years to come.

Ashlee began dating in high school. She had her first serious girlfriend when she was sixteen. There were a few others as well, one of whom she became romantically involved with. The other focus in her life was the family business, a bakery. At first grandparents, parents, and aunts and uncles all participated in this business. But there were issues among the family members, and as time went on, her parents became the sole proprietors. The expectation was that Ashlee would run the bakery once she graduated from high school. But she had other plans by then; she wanted to go to college.

College, at Stony Brook on Long Island, opened up a whole new world to Ashlee. For the first time in her life she was not the only Asian. In fact, Stony Brook was a melting pot that embraced diversity. Ashlee was meeting kids from high schools that boasted graduating classes of five or six or even seven hundred students, people who were used to mixed-ethnicity communities and did not see her as being an outsider just because she was Asian—though her Celtic/Polish name still raised a few eyebrows.

Ashlee studied statistics and economics. To appease her parents, she went home on some weekends to spend long hours (beginning at 2:00 a.m.) at the bakery. But when she was at Stony Brook, she took advantage of other sorts of opportunities, including the chance to finally learn something about the Korean culture. One of her roommates, Norm, was a fellow Korean, born in the United States to Korean parents. He took her to Manhattan to taste Korean food for the first time in his parents' restaurant. Ashlee loved it immediately. (While many people cringe at the smell of kimchi, it smelled and tasted familiar to her. She learned that in Korea many people believe in feeding children a sweeter version of normally spicy kimchi early on so they'll be used to it when they get older.) While Norm's brother was hoping to become more Americanized, Norm himself was intent on staying connected to his heritage. His enthusiasm for Korean culture was a boon for Ashlee. For the first time she was able to envision herself as a person with roots.

In spite of all these new experiences, Ashlee didn't meet anyone from the LGBT community. Stony Brook had one, but Ashlee was doing her best to try to fit in as she was—or as she appeared to be. She found that there were times in her life when she could suppress her true feelings, when she could tell herself, "Thinking of yourself as a woman is not normal; people will think of you differently if you don't behave normally." She did her best to lock that part of herself away and enjoy the new adventures that had been thrown at her feet. And enjoy herself she did, sometimes too much. Her new friends liked to party. For the first year and a half Ashlee concentrated more on college culture than on her studies. But after that she straightened out and applied herself. Postgraduation, she accepted a job as a business analyst for an insurance company in Connecticut. That's where she met her future wife, Holly.

Holly was Korean as well; she was also adopted, in her case into an Italian family. Like Ashlee, she had grown up in a rural community (in Connecticut) where she had no exposure to Korean culture. Ashlee probably wasn't the best person to share her secondhand knowledge of the culture, but their backgrounds alone—Holly worked for the same insurance company where Ashlee had found herself—offered them a secure foundation on which to build a relationship.

The couple decided early on that they didn't want children. But as time went by they had a change of heart. It was then they learned there were some complications and in fact they were not likely to be able to have children. Around this time Ashlee had an opportunity to continue her work for the same insurance company in another city: Atlanta. Ashlee and Holly wanted the experience of living in another part of the country, so they moved. Holly underwent surgery in Atlanta to determine if the removal of some cysts might pave the way for a pregnancy; it might have, but they wouldn't ever find that out.

In 2014, Holly left Georgia to be with her mother, who was very ill. She stayed in Connecticut caretaking for several months, until her mother passed away. The separation was actually a good thing, because Ashlee and Holly had been experiencing some marital challenges, and Ashlee needed the time alone to think. It was while Holly was gone that Ashlee decided she had to tell Holly the truth about herself. She didn't want to hit Holly with it as soon as she got home, but she knew she couldn't wait too much longer. The time had come.

In September of that year, Ashlee came out to her wife. Ashlee could only tell her so much, because she only knew so much herself. She didn't even know if she would transition; she hadn't thought that far into the future. She only knew that she felt the need to go out into the world a few times a month presenting that part of herself that she had long kept under lock and key. She had no idea where her journey would lead, only that it had begun.

Holly asked a lot of questions, but after they were answered to the best of Ashlee's ability, she shut down, as was her way, to analyze the information she'd been given. It was a bad time for her generally. Not only had she recently lost her mother, but her father was dead too. She had no siblings, no relatives at all really, other than one aunt. They hadn't been in Atlanta that long. They hadn't made any good friends yet. She wasn't working. She had nothing to latch on to. Holly was isolated, alone, and scared, feelings that Ashlee could well relate to.

In January of 2015, Ashlee attended the First Event transgender conference in Waltham, Massachusetts. There she was able to catch up with some people she'd gotten to know back in Connecticut. Some had transitioned, some were in the process, and some were still deciding whether or not they could. It was a great experience for Ashlee to be able to hear about their various journeys. While at the conference she attended a few workshops and learned from presenting doctors about the array of medical procedures available for people who were thinking of transitioning. She got some quotes, though she still only half believed she would ever use them.

In March of that year, Ashlee attended the Keystone Transgender Conference in Harrisburg, Pennsylvania, and met with yet more physicians and received more quotes, for facial feminization surgery (FFS) and breast augmentation (BA). Her need to be herself, she realized, was escalating quickly. When she got home she told Holly that she planned to begin hormone therapy. Holly was supportive, but the anxiety in her voice and on her face was evident.

Not long after Ashlee joined a transgender support group. This gave her the chance to hear yet more stories from people in various stages of transition. She felt herself relating to their struggles, and their successes when goals were met. A lot of them seemed to be in a hurry to make their transitions. Ashlee knew she would have to set her own pace for her own transition; it had to serve both her and Holly.

One of the support groups' visiting physicians was someone Ashlee felt comfortable with. She made an appointment with her in September 2015 so that she could begin hormone replacement therapy (HRT). The physician referred her to a therapist to make sure she was a candidate for the treatments. Two months later Ashlee began HRT, which seemed to surprise Holly, who had known the time was coming but had expected it would be a few years out. Ashlee's therapist invited Holly to come in some appointments, to get a better understanding of what was happening. This seemed to help superficially, but Ashlee knew that down deep Holly was unable to express her fears about the way her life was unraveling. Ashlee had a lifetime to come to terms with who she was; Holly had less than a year to process the information. Holly didn't want to be a lesbian; she didn't want to be thought of as one. She didn't want things to change.

In February of 2016, Ashlee made the decision to transition at work on October 11, which is National Coming Out Day. Setting a date made it easier for her to put together a plan to tell her employer, friends, family, and neighbors in advance of that date. But it made things harder than ever for Holly, who was about to lose, as far as she was concerned, the person she been with for the last eleven years. Over the next months, Ashlee began the arduous task of having conversations with people about her decision. In August she made a trip to Connecticut to tell the people there. Holly accompanied her. The process of coming out over and over again to different individuals was extremely hard at first, but after a while it got easier; Ashlee began to feel "lighter" with the message she had to deliver. It helped that virtually all the people she talked to were supportive. By the time she told her colleagues at work, she felt somewhat empowered by the encouragement she'd received to date. Her office was a big one—with a total of 115 people and 30 more working remotely. Many of them were younger creative types who offered their acceptance right away. And everyone was courteous and willing to use the right pronouns. Ashlee appreciated their support. She understood that it would be an adjustment for them.

Unfortunately, Ashlee was not able to tell her mother. She was driving up to visit with her and considering telling her, although her mother was quite ill by then and Ashlee didn't know if her mother would be able to take the information in. But when Ashlee arrived and realized how close to death her mother was, she decided not to say anything; she didn't want her last words to her mother to be about herself. She didn't tell her father right away, because he was losing his wife and then grieving her death. But she knew when the time came that he would be supportive. He had been stern when he was younger; now he was much more in touch with his feelings. Besides, Stephanie had paved the way with her own revelations.

Although Ashlee's marriage is still up in the air as of this writing (Holly recently asked for a divorce), Ashlee's journey has brought her clarity. It has taught her the importance of knowing who you are and giving yourself permission to look and act accordingly. It has also taught her to appreciate her cultural heritage. (While Ashlee does not pretend to be expert when it comes to Korean cuisine, she has mastered dishes like kalbi, japchae, pajeon, jaeyook kimchi bokum—and Korean spaghetti, an "insider" dish—angel hair pasta, Spam kimchi, and spices—not found on Korean restaurant menus.)

From Linda's Office

Though Ashlee grew up in the United States, she was born in Korea, and both her biological parents were Korean. Accordingly, her hair and skin have different characteristics than that of the other people included here. Ashlee has been undergoing laser treatments for over two years, and her facial hair is about 90 to 95 percent cleared. She's had fifteen treatments on her face and nine over the rest of my body, which is 95 percent cleared. She had no back or chest hair to worry about. Her arms had very little hair and only needed a little thinning. As of this writing she has only three full body treatments left.

Debora

"I've Tried to Cure, Deny, Outgrow, or Just Stoically Endure and Grow Too Old to Care about It Anymore. The Problem with All Those Strategies Was That I Was Fundamentally Projecting a Lie."

When you are forced to lie to yourself and others, you become emotionally isolated and unable to participate wholly in your experience of life. This is what happened to Debora over the course of her first forty years as she tried to be the best man she could be. She was so earnest that even the woman in her life, whom she eventually married (and ultimately divorced), was optimistic that Debora's less masculine inclinations would come to an end, that marriage itself would implement stability. So Debora married. She was already a bodybuilder, a rock climber, a spelunker, and a diver. She'd gone all out to compensate for how she felt on the inside.

Debora hadn't gotten married to get "cured," but she had felt confident that marriage *would* cure her. So she was surprised to find when she awoke each morning that she was unchanged. Her wife was a PhD, an engineer, masculine in her attitude, very smart, sincere but also emotionally withdrawn. When she saw that Debora's internal dilemmas persisted, she took it as a knock against her own femininity. She felt threatened. She became even more determined to make herself woman enough for the man she had married.

Together Debora and her wife sought to fix—or at least contain—the situation. Debora tried one coping mechanism after another (including therapy and even guidance from her church).

Nothing worked, and eventually it was clear that suicide ideation, anger, and hurt would only persist and further impede her ability to function as a father and husband. Debora's wife gave her six months to figure out what she wanted to do. When the six months were up, Debora professed her desire to transition, and the divorce was initiated.

Debora's wife gave her a week to get out. This meant she had a week to tell their children, daughters ages fifteen and twelve and a son who was nine. The kids, who had always enjoyed a loving and protective family life, went from a state of oblivion regarding their parents' problems to the realization that they would no longer have a father in the house. Debora's son tried his best to cure Debora. Her middle child was just coming to terms with her own femininity; she felt in some way that the person she had known as her dad was mimicking her, and she withdrew. Debora's eldest daughter became aggressive and belligerent in her grief. That was a year ago as of this writing. Debora has worked hard to explain her needs and resolve issues. Her son has now offered acceptance, her middle daughter has become less withdrawn, and her older daughter is moving into something akin to acceptance.

Debora had eight months to make the transition at work. Her job entails the marketing of chemicals, and she has an international clientele. She travels frequently. When she was with her kids, for a time, she still presented herself as male. At work she still presented as male too, but she tried to dress in clothing that might be suitable for either sex. Still, it was not easy. There were mornings when it took her two hours to get dressed, and it could be absolutely dispiriting to stand in front of the mirror after all that time and realize she didn't know the person staring back at her. But her colleagues, who were used to thinking of her as a guy, still saw her that way. If we perceive someone as masculine, Debora suggests, we mentally exaggerate their male features. When she was out somewhere among strangers and wearing the same androgynous clothing, people called her ma'am or miss. Debora looked forward to getting her new identification documents and moving fully into her new life.

Seventy-five percent of transgender people don't have sex reassignment surgery. As Debora explains, it is only a small part of being a trans person. The transition happens foremost in your head and in your heart. The preoccupation with surgery is part of a transgender narrative that has been created by various vendors who service transgender communities. The thinking is that if a woman is trapped in a man's body, she needs to go under the knife as soon as possible in order to set herself free.

At first, Debora did not want to talk about SRS. She was still learning about herself and her needs. As she explains, it's not like you know from childhood that you are a girl in a boy's body. Reality is much more subtle. You know something is wrong, but when you are five or six or seven, the world is your parents and everything that happens in the house and school. Whatever the adults in your life perceive as the norm is what you perceive as the norm. It would take tremendous self-knowledge for a young child to work against the grain of parents and teachers. Some kids do, but most don't. They just know their brain is mismatched to the circumstances they find themselves in. So they try to fit in. When they succeed to some extent, they experience imposter syndrome symptoms. They may become depressed and alienated. But at some point, a light goes off. Finally they have a clue as to what is wrong. "Who do I see myself as when I close my eyes?" they may ask themselves. That is the seed, and from the seed, the tree begins to grow. How big it will get and in what way it will develop is different for each individual. Some men may say to themselves, "I'm going to continue to present as a male and do my best," while others will say, "I am a woman, and I must make changes to be consistent." What those changes entail is a matter of personal choice and will differ from one person to another.

Debora has had hormone therapy, and while she admits that it has had some impact on the chemistry of her mind (as well as her body), the greater determinant has been her decision to begin her transition in the first place. Once, after she had begun her transition but before she even started hormone therapy, she spent some time chatting with a man whom she found intriguing, and before they parted, he asked her for a kiss. In that moment, the moment of the kiss, it was as if she had lived in a shack all her life, a small space with no light, and now the walls exploded and she found herself standing under a bright sun surrounded by green grass and rolling meadows. In that moment she understood what it was like to be a woman experiencing a sexual attraction for a man.

Debora was nineteen or twenty before she had the confidence to start researching "transgender." As the oldest boy in a three-sibling family, she had always felt the need to be surrogate dad to her younger brother when her own father, who was loving but who drank and had affairs, was not around. Her mom was often preoccupied trying to keep the marriage together, and when Debora tried to confide in her about her confusion over any identity issues, her mother would only tease her and make a joke of her concerns.

Debora was the kind of child who lived in her head. She was always thinking, and she learned early on to hide what she was thinking. She was not at liberty to be herself. Perhaps that's why she started stuttering badly. When she was bullied by the other kids, she fell back on her I'm-smarter-than-you strategy. No one could get close enough to know who she really was.

Even later, as an adult who had come to full knowledge, it was difficult to begin to act on her inclinations. It takes time to get strength, Debora warns. In the beginning, everyone turns against you. Your family turns against you. All your support structures crumble. The world is suddenly full of wolves, and you are naked and alone. In many ways it is another form of bullying, such as she endured as a kid. Bullying is the way in which the world releases its anger, she says, at anyone who is different or emotionally weak. We want everyone to be clear; we want feminine women and masculine men. You have to be very strong. And after a time, people come around. They may not "get it," but they find they can love you anyway.

Debora has not sought out transgender support groups. She struggles to see herself that way. She is Debora; she *is* a woman. She has a therapist, and she has more friends now than she has ever had. Her new friends see her as she really is. She is also a practicing Christian and a Sunday school teacher. Christianity, Debora explains, was something she came to as a teen. She thought being "born again" might cure her of wanting to be a woman. She went to extremes, even to the point of speaking in tongues. Today she is more moderate but still a believer. As someone who has studied science as well as the Bible, she is able to interpret Biblical passages through her understanding of how the world works.

How one is perceived is almost always important to people in transition. When Debora is dressed as a women and sees a guy smirking at her, as if he sees her as a man, it can produce intense feelings of unhappiness. Fortunately, she doesn't look much like a guy anymore. Even as a kid she was always smaller than everyone else. She started puberty late, and the associated hair growth didn't begin until she was in her late teens. In her high school photo she looks like a twelve-year-old surrounded by adults. With electrolysis, hormones, and lucky genetics, her facial skin is smooth, and she doesn't call undue attention to herself; she can function as a standard-issue woman in society. But not every transgender woman can. The world will have to shift in its perceptions, Debora says.

Debora eventually completed her transition. She remained successful in the same career she had previously and restored her relationship with her children. She lives as a happy, successful, and single woman. Her next adventures will be in dating, but she is in no rush.

From Linda's Office

Debora started hair removal in her midforties. We have worked with her for a period of four years to date. Her hair is a mix of black, brown, red, and blonde, and it includes both coarse and fine textures.

We began Debora's sessions with laser hair removal on her face, which required about 4,590 laser zaps over the course of her first year with us. (An average of about 300 zaps can be performed in one session working on the face and depending on the individual person.) Her laser work cost her $1,860.

Debora needed electrolysis after her laser work to deal with the facial hairs that would not respond to laser. This required an additional thirty hours, or 1,800 minutes, at a cost of about $2,550.

Debora's general body work required 14,543 laser zaps for a cost of $2,045.

Debora's SRS prep work has taken about twelve hours over a period of five months. She came in two or three times a month. We are currently working on clearing away oddball hairs. For the most part, she is done. Cost about $1,045.

All told, Debora has undergone forty-two treatments for electrolysis and another forty for laser work, for a total of eighty-two treatments at a cost of about $7,500.

From Debora's Blog:

Natural-born citizens are seen as inherently more real than an immigrant; an immigrant had choices, another country, and thus potentially still holds other allegiances. The natural-born citizen has only ever known one country, can only have one civic identity, and is thus seen as inherently more trustworthy.

This is of course false, as an immigrant had choices, yes, and chose their adopted country, paying the cost of loss of friends, family, and national identity and often experiencing being displaced and starting all over again. Their love for their adopted country is all the more sincere as it's an informed and costly one. Their citizenship is not by mere accident of birth, but by costly choice.

The same holds for trans people. We've soul-searched, found our identity, forfeited our old genders to identify with the new one, started from scratch, and, just like an immigrant with an accent, faced constant discrimination by being unable to hide where we came from, and persisted until we obtained citizenship. Our love and identity is not by accident of birth. It's an informed, cold choice. A costly choice. And we love who we are with everything we have.

Glossary of Transgender, Nonbinary and Genderqueer Words

The extensive glossary that follows is adapted from Anagnori, who describes him/herself as an "asexual, aromantic, nonbinary trans person." Anagnori's website, found at Anagnori. Tumblr.com, offers visitors all kinds of great information, including essays, help, advice, resources, and much more. We highly recommend it to everyone reading these pages. We were not able to find a contact for Anagnori, who only asks people copying information from his/her website to credit him/her, so we could not thank him/her personally. Anagnori, thank you very much for contributing, albeit unwittingly, to this book.

The following glossary is a resource for people who are looking for more information about trans terminology, whether they are confused, searching, or merely curious.

Pronouns are not listed here, because they vary so much across individuals. Always follow a person's wishes regarding the pronouns you use for them.

For brevity's sake, I use "trans" as an umbrella term for trans men, trans women, and all nonbinary, genderqueer, and gender-variant identities, but in practice not all people in those groups identify as trans. No disrespect or identity policing is intended by this.

This list is heavily Anglo-centric because I am not qualified to define or translate terms that originate outside of Western English-speaking culture. I have included a few of those terms because I've seen them pop up in Western discussions of gender occasionally, but be warned that they're only the tip of the iceberg.

There's a huge amount of diversity that I do not know enough about to include here.

This glossary is supposed to be descriptive, not prescriptive. It covers a small "snapshot" of how these words were used by the trans communities I was involved in at one point in time. It is not supposed to be used to tell people what words *should* mean or to limit the way that people can use and change these words. Language is always changing, and glossaries like this will always be inadequate to fit everyone's needs. People will use these words in ways not mentioned in my list, and that does not make their identities or experiences any less valid. Thus, this list will always be incomplete and a little out of date.

AFAB: Assigned female at birth.

Agender, Agendered: A nonbinary identity meaning without a gender or gender identity.

Alia, Aliagender: "A gender experience which is 'other,' or stands apart from existing gender constructs" (from askanonbinary).

AMAB: Assigned male at birth.

Ambigender: 1. Available or common to more than one gender. 2. A nonbinary identity related to androgyne, bigender, and/or genderfluid.

Androgens: Hormones such as testosterone, sometimes called "male sex hormones," although people of any gender can have high androgen levels, and not all men have high androgen levels.

Androgyne: A nonbinary identity meaning a combination, blending, or in-between point between two genders (usually between male and female). Androgynes may or may not present androgynously and may or may not experience multiple genders.

Androgynous, Androgyny: 1. Related to an androgyne gender identity. 2. A gender presentation that is ambiguous between male and female, or which blends them, or lies in the middle between them.

Androgynous of Center: Any of several gender identities that lean closer to "androgyne" than to male or female.

Androsexual: Sexually attracted to masculinity or to men. Warning: this word is sometimes used in transphobic ways.

Antiandrogens: Drugs that negate the effects of testosterone, usually given during adolescence to trans youth who do not wish to develop conventionally "masculine" features. A type of hormone blocker.

Antiestrogens: Drugs that negate the effects of estradiol and other estrogens, usually given during adolescence to trans youth who do not wish to develop conventionally "feminine" features. A type of hormone blocker.

ASAB: Assigned sex at birth.

Assigned Sex (At Birth): The gender identity imposed on someone by their family and by society. This gender is usually decided at birth or in utero and is usually based on genitalia. Almost all people are assigned male or female at birth, even if they are intersex.

Autoandrophilia: Pleasure, sexual or otherwise, derived from imagining oneself as a man. The much rarer counterpart to autogynephilia, and also not recommended.

Autogynephilia: Pleasure, sexual or otherwise, derived from imagining oneself as a woman. Historically, diagnosis of autogynephilia was/is commonly used to restrict trans women's access to transitioning and to pathologize them as mentally ill. Not recommended for general discourse.

Being Read: An alternative phrase to "passing" that shifts responsibility of correct gendering onto onlookers, instead of on the person who is read. A trans person who is read correctly is recognized as their correct gender.

Bigender: A nonbinary identity in which a person has two or more genders. Any combination of genders is possible, not just male/female. These genders may be present simultaneously, they may fluctuate, or both.

Binarism: The belief, prejudice, or social force that claims only two genders exist, male and female, and that all nonbinary and genderqueer gender identities are invalid. Binarism is inextricably tied to colonialism and racism and is a way that Western European cultures attack the gender expression of other cultures and ethnic groups.

Binary Gender: A gender that is either strictly male or strictly female. This is not affected by whether a person is cis or trans: a trans man or trans woman has a binary gender unless he or she also identifies as nonbinary.

Binder: In trans discussions, a garment used to minimize or alter the appearance of breasts.

Binding: The practice of hiding or reshaping breasts, usually to achieve a more masculine or androgynous appearance.

Biological Essentialism: In trans discussions, the belief that a person's gender can only be defined by their genes and/or genitalia at birth. Biological essentialism usually ignores the existence of intersex people and is a major component of transphobia.

Biological Sex: A social construct that categorizes human bodies as male or female based on chromosomes or genitalia. Contrary to popular belief, there are not two biological sexes, because people can be born with a wide variety of sexual characteristics and many different combinations of sexual characteristics. Many trans and/or intersex people find the phrase or concept offensive and prefer the phrase "assigned sex" or "designated sex."

Body Dysphoria: A feeling of stress or unhappiness related to one's body. In trans discussions, it is a type of gender dysphoria caused by the body's appearance clashing with one's internal gender identity.

Bottom Surgery: A colloquial term for surgery that corrects one's genitalia to better match one's preferred gender presentation.

Brain Sex: A controversial idea that posits that a person's gender identity may be reflected by the structure of their brain.

Butch: More reminiscent of what is traditionally considered boyish or masculine than feminine. May refer to a gender identity, gender presentation, or a style of dress. Often associated with lesbian culture.

CAFAB: Coercively assigned female at birth.

CAMAB: Coercively assigned male at birth.

CASAB: Coercively assigned sex at birth. *See* assigned sex at birth.

Cis: Short for cisgender or cissexual.

Cis Privilege: Short for cisgender privilege.

Cisgender: Consistently experiencing your gender in a way that matches the gender assigned to you at birth. Not trans.

Cisgender Privilege: The benefits, opportunities, and everyday courtesies that cisgender people are able to take for granted, and which trans and nonbinary people may not be able to count on.

Cishet: A person who is cisgender, heteroromantic, and heterosexual.

Cissexism: The unjust social institution that validates cisgender identities more than trans identities and which grants privileges to cis people while oppressing trans people.

Cissexual: Usually a synonym for cisgender, though some people make a distinction, similar to the transgender/transsexual distinction.

Chaser: A person who seeks out trans people for dating or sex. Chasers have a bad reputation for fetishizing, disrespecting, and mistreating trans people, especially trans women.

Chromosomes: Gene sequences that determine how an organism's body develops and reproduces. The human sex chromosomes, X and Y, usually determine whether a fetus develops typical egg-producing anatomy or typical sperm-producing anatomy. However, other factors can affect a person's anatomical and psychological development, and the chromosomes do not necessarily reflect a person's true gender.

Clocking: An event in which an observer notices or realizes a trans person's assigned sex at birth without the trans person's consent.

Colonialism: In trans discussions, colonialism is the practice of imposing Western systems of gender onto non-Western cultures, invalidating native people's gender identities in the process. Colonialism can involve either denying that a gender exists or reinterpreting the gender to fit a Western model, e.g., by claiming that a hijra person must be transgender. Binarism is a form of colonialism.

Coming Out: In trans discussions, the process of telling someone that one is trans. This applies both to trans people who have transitioned to live as their correct gender as well as to those who have not.

Correct Pronouns: Alternate phrase for "preferred pronouns."

Corrective Rape: Sexual assault done with the intent to change someone's sexual or romantic orientation or gender identity. Trans people, especially trans women and sex workers, are sometimes victimized by corrective rape.

Cross-Dresser: A person who chooses to wear clothing that does not match their gender identity or usual gender presentation. A controversial concept because clothing is not intrinsically gendered, and the wearer may define it as appropriate to their own gender regardless of social norms. This is a loaded term and should not be used without the permission of the person being referred to.

Cross-Dressing: The act of wearing clothing that does not match one's gender identity. A controversial concept because clothing is not intrinsically gendered, and the wearer may define it as appropriate to their own gender regardless of social norms. Trans people who wear the clothing of their assigned sex may consider themselves as cross-dressing; when wearing clothing of their actual gender, they are *not* cross-dressing, though they may appear that way to uninformed people.

Crossplay: To dress up as a fictional or historical character that is of a different gender than oneself. A controversial concept because clothing is not intrinsically gendered, and the wearer may define it as appropriate to their own gender regardless of social norms.

Deep Stealth: Living full time as one's correct gender, without any of the people one regularly interacts with knowing that one is trans.

Degender: To ignore or invalidate someone's gender. Similar to misgendering but does not necessarily impose a different, inaccurate gender onto the target person while invalidating them.

Dehumanization: A kind of stigma that lessens a person by making them seem less than human; often likening them to an animal, machine, or monster. A common component of transphobia.

Demiboy: *See* demiguy.

Demienby: A gender that is partly one nonbinary gender and partly another nonbinary gender.

Demigender: Umbrella term for demigirl, demiguy, demienby, demiboy, and similar genders.

Demigirl: A gender that is partly female and partly nonbinary. Can be AFAB or AMAB.

Demiguy: A gender that is partly male and partly nonbinary. Can be AMAB or AFAB.

Detransition: To stop, pause, or reverse some or all of the effects of transitioning.

DFAB: Designated female at birth. Alternative to AFAB.

Desexualization: A stigma that denies a person's sexuality or sexual agency. A common component of transphobia.

Designated Sex (At Birth): An alternative phrase for assigned sex at birth.

DMAB: Designated male at birth. Alternative to AMAB.

Drag: Cross-dressing. Drag is done for a wide variety of reasons and purposes. People in drag may attempt to plausibly appear as their target gender, parody gender, exaggerate gender, or deconstruct gender. Some people who wear drag are trans, and some are not. *See* cross-dressing for problematic elements of this concept.

Drag King: A person who does not identify as male but dresses up to resemble one. Trans men are *not* drag kings, because they are men. However, some people who appear to be drag kings may later come to identify as trans men. *See* cross-dressing for problematic elements of this concept.

Drag Queen: A person who does not identify as female but dresses up to resemble one. Trans women are *not* drag queens, because they are women. However, some people who appear to be drag queens may later come to identify as trans women. *See* cross-dressing for problematic elements of this concept.

DSM: The Diagnostic and Statistical Manual of Mental Disorders. The DSM-IV includes Gender Identity Disorder, which was re-named Gender Dysphoria in the DSM-V. There is controversy over whether these ideas should be included in the DSM or not.

Dysphoria: In trans discussions, a feeling of displeasure, stress, anxiety, or depression related to one's gender. *See* gender dysphoria.

Dyadic: Having a stereotypically male or female anatomy, as Western culture would define it; not intersex.

Electrolysis: Permanent hair removal. Sometimes taken by trans people to achieve a better gender presentation or feel more comfortable in their bodies.

Enby: Casual term for a nonbinary person. Not all nonbinary people want to be referred to as enbies, so individual preferences should be respected here.

Endocrinologist: A doctor who specializes in hormones. Trans people may need to see endocrinologists as they transition.

Epicene: An archaic term for someone who has characteristics of both genders or who can't be classified as purely male or female. Most often used for male-assigned people with feminine tendencies. Like most of these older terms, you shouldn't refer to someone this way unless they give you permission.

Erasure: A lack of representation of a group in media, news, and pop culture. Erasure may be either deliberate or accidental and targets all queer identities to varying degrees.

Estradiol: The most potent and common form of estrogen in the human body. Supplemental estradiol is sometimes taken by trans people, usually with the intent of achieving a more feminine appearance.

Estrogens: Hormones such as estradiol. Sometimes called "female hormones," although people of any gender can have high levels of estrogens, and not all women have high estrogen levels.

Eunuch: A man whose penis has been removed or (rarely) a man who has been sterilized. This term should not be used to refer to trans people.

FAAB: Female-assigned at birth. Alternative to AFAB.

Female-Bodied: A common but problematic term used for cis women and AFAB trans people who have not undergone transitional surgery. AFAB and DFAB are recommended instead.

Feminine of Center: Having a gender that is closer to "female" than to "male" or other genders.

Femme: Reminiscent of what is traditionally considered femininity. May refer to a gender identity, gender presentation, or a style of dress. Strongly associated with lesbian culture.

Fluid: Changeable, not static. Some people have fluid sexual orientations or gender identities. *See* genderfluid.

FTM, F2M: Female to male.

FTN, F2N: Female to neutral.

FTX, F2X: Female to an unspecified gender.

Full Time: Living as one's correct gender every day, in all circumstances, in a way publicly visible to all people. Gatekeepers often require a period of living full time before they are willing to approve of hormone therapy or surgery; this restriction can be dangerous or impossible for some trans people.

Gaff: Underwear used for tucking. Sometimes used by DMAB trans people.

Gatekeepers: People who have the power to progress or halt a trans person's journey of transition. These can include doctors, government officials, employers, family members, and more.

Gender: *n.* A person's internal mental experience of themself and their relationship to "male," "female," "androgynous," "genderless," and other identities. It is distinct from a person's assigned sex, anatomy, gender presentation, pronouns, socialization, and sexual orientation. Some people do not have a gender.

Gender: *v.* To treat someone as if they are of a particular gender. This takes many forms, the most common of which are pronouns.

Gender Affirmation Surgery: Surgery that alters a person's appearance to better reflect their preferred gender presentation. Also called gender confirmation surgery.

Gender Bender, Gender Bending: 1. Altering or playing with gender presentation. 2. In fiction, changing either a character's gender identity, gender presentation, or both. A problematic concept because it tends to conflate gender identity with gender presentation or assigned sex.

Gender Binary: The Western social construct that only grants legitimacy to two genders, male and female. Is frequently oppressive toward people who are trans and/or intersex.

Gender Confirmation Surgery: Surgery that alters a person's appearance to better reflect their preferred gender presentation. Also called gender affirmation surgery.

Gender Diversity: The inclusion of many or all genders, not just male and female.

Gender Dysphoria: 1. A feeling of discomfort, stress, confusion, or negativity that is caused by a mismatch between one's assigned sex and one's actual gender. Can be either body dysphoria, social dysphoria, or both. Many trans and/or nonbinary people experience gender dysphoria, but not all do. 2. The phrase used for transgender experiences in the DSM-V.

Gender Identity Disorder: The phrase used for transgender experiences in the DSM-IV.

Gender Essentialism: The belief that there are intrinsic and unchangeable differences between genders and that these differences manifest as anatomy, chromosomes, behavior, socialization, and/or gender roles. A key component of transphobia.

Gender Expression: The speech, clothing, body modification choices, gestures, behavior, and social roles through which a person demonstrates their gender.

Gender Neutral: Not specific or restricted to any particular gender.

Gender Neutral Language: The use of nouns, titles, and pronouns in such a way as to avoid specifying gender. This is useful for making environments and discussions more accessible to trans and nonbinary people.

Gender Nonconformity: Acting, speaking, or dressing in a manner that is not traditionally encouraged for members of one's gender.

Gender Norm: An arbitrary expectation or standard that is applied to people of a certain gender.

Gender Presentation: The way that a person's gender superficially appears to onlookers, which may be affected by anatomy, clothing, makeup, hairstyle, speech patterns, and body language. May also include a person's stated desire to be treated as a certain gender and referred to with certain pronouns.

Gender Reassignment Surgery: An older term for gender affirmation surgery or gender confirmation surgery. It is rather inaccurate because the surgery does not change the recipient's gender but alters the body to better reflect the gender.

Gender Role: A set of expectations, standards, and cultural pressures associated with a particular gender. People may freely choose to follow or disregard gender roles. Conformity to gender roles does not reflect a person's actual gender; cis people who violate gender roles do not become trans, nor do trans people need to follow traditional gender roles in order for their genders to be valid.

Gender-Variant: 1. Behaving or presenting one's gender in a way that does not fit traditional models of male or female. 2. An umbrella term, similar to nonbinary and genderqueer.

Genderflexible: *See* genderfluid.

Genderfluid: Having a gender that is changeable. Genderfluid people may shift between multiple genders over time or feel gender in different ways over time. Their preferred pronouns and gender presentation may or may not reflect these changes. Related to but distinct from genderflux.

Genderflux: Having a gender that varies in intensity or degree over time. Related to but distinct from genderfluid.

Genderfuck: Gender presentation that deliberately seeks to violate conventional standards of male or female presentation.

Genderless: Without a gender or gender identity. Similar to agender.

Genderqueer: 1. An umbrella term that includes all gender identities other than strictly male or strictly female. Covers the same set of people as "nonbinary," but it has different social and political connotations and is more strongly associated with "queering gender" and the queer political movement. 2. Gender presentation that is not strictly male or female.

Genetic Sex: *See* biological sex.

Graygender, Greygender: A person who identifies as (at least partially) outside the gender binary and has a strong natural ambivalence about their gender identity or gender expression. Coined by invernom.

GSD: Gender and sexual diversity. *See* GSM.

GSM, GSRM: Gender, sexual, and romantic minorities. An alternative acronym to LGBT+.

Gynecomastia: Uncommonly large breast tissue in nonfemale persons.

Gynosexual: Sexually attracted to femininity or to women. This word has also been wrongly used to mean "attracted to women with vaginas," and to thus exclude trans women. (Note that *gyno-* is a prefix meaning "woman," not "vagina.") Because of this, many trans people do not like this word.

Harry Benjamin Syndrome: An outdated term for transgender or transsexual experiences. Not recommended because of problematic associations about what constitutes "true" transsexuality.

HBS: Harry Benjamin Syndrome.

Hermaphrodite: A creature with both male and female sexual characteristics. This term should not be applied to humans.

Heteronormativity: The cultural force that expects all people to be cisgender, heteroromantic, and heterosexual. Major problem that affects all queer identities, including asexuals. Closely linked to homophobia, biphobia, transphobia, and acephobia.

Heterosexism: *See* heteronormativity.

Hormone Blockers: Drugs used to negate or prevent the effects of hormones, particularly sex hormones. These include antiandrogens and antiestrogens. Also called puberty blockers, puberty suppressors, puberty inhibitors, or hormone suppressors.

Hormone Replacement Therapy: Therapy in which a person is given hormones that their body lacks or does not have enough of. Many, but not all, trans people choose to use hormones to alter their gender presentation. Some cis people also undergo hormone replacement therapy for other purposes, e.g. estrogen replacement for postmenopausal women.

HRT: Hormone replacement therapy.

Hypersexualization: Treating a person as highly or overly sexual, or sexually objectifying them, at the cost of respecting them as a person. Commonly done by chasers and trans fetishists to trans people, especially trans women.

Identity Policing: Telling a person that the way they identify or the labels they use to describe themselves are wrong.

Internalization: The unconscious process in which a person accepts society's values and applies them to themself. Internalized homophobia, misogyny, cissexism, and transphobia can hinder a person's understanding and acceptance of their gender.

Intersex: Born with anatomy or genetics that do not easily fit into the Western cultural stereotypes of "male bodies" or "female bodies." This should not be considered a defect or disorder. Intersex people can be cisgender or transgender and of any gender identity. There are many ways that a person can be intersex.

Intergender: A gender identity that is particularly intended for intersex people to use.

Invalidation: In trans discussions, a refusal to acknowledge someone's gender as real and worthy of respect, or to acknowledge the value of their experiences.

LGBT+: Lesbian, gay, bisexual, transgender, and others. An acronym for the cultural and political community of people who are not heterosexual, heteroromantic, and cisgender. Sometimes expanded up to LGBT*QQIAUP+, in which T* = all transgender, nonbinary, and genderqueer people; Q = queer/questioning; I = intersex; A = asexual; U = undecided; and P = pansexual.

MAAB: Male-assigned at birth. Alternative to AMAB.

Male-Bodied: A common but problematic term used for cis men and AMAB trans people who have not undergone transitional surgery. AMAB and DMAB are recommended instead.

Masculine of Center: Having a gender that is closer to "male" than to "female" or other genders.

Masculinization: 1. The process by which a person's gender presentation becomes closer to what is traditionally considered masculine. 2. In fetal development, the process by which androgen hormones affect the developing brain.

Misgender: To treat someone as the incorrect gender.

Mispronoun: To misgender someone by using an incorrect pronoun for them.

MTF, M2F: Male to female.

MTN, M2N: Male to neutral.

MTX, M2X: Male to an unspecified gender.

Multigender: An umbrella term for all people with multiple genders, including bigender, trigender, polygender, and pangender, as well as genderfluid people who identify as multigender.

Mx.: A gender-neutral honorific, analogous to Mr. or Ms.

Natal Man/Woman: A cisgender man or woman. This term is sometimes used by transphobic people to invalidate trans people, and as such, it is not recommended.

Neutrois: 1. Having a gender that is specifically neutral, or a neutral third gender that is neither male nor female. 2. Without a gender or gender identity, similar to agender. 3. A form of gender presentation without prominent sexual characteristics.

No Gender: Without a gender or gender identity. *See also* agender and genderless.

Nonbinary: 1. Any gender, or lack of gender, or mix of genders that is not strictly male or female. 2. "Nonbinary is a term for people who are not men or women, or are both men and women, or who are something else entirely, or are some combination of these things, or some of these things some of the time." —askanonbinary

Nongendered: Without a gender or gender identity. Similar to agender and genderless.

Packer: A prosthetic penis or similar tool, often used by trans men and transmasculine AFAB people.

Packing: The act of using a packer.

Pangender: Having or experiencing all genders, or many genders, either simultaneously or over time; may also include an agender or genderless experience. (Note: This term may have racist/colonialist implications if a person uses it to claim an identity from a culture they are not part of or are not treating with respect.)

Passing: The state of being perceived as the gender one wishes to be seen as.

Pathologization: The act of treating something as an illness or disorder that is abnormal and needs to be fixed. Transgender status is often pathologized, especially for trans women.

Polygender: Having or experiencing several genders, either simultaneously or over time; may also include an agender or genderless experience.

Preferred Pronouns: The pronouns that a person wishes to be called by. Using a person's preferred pronouns is a key part of respecting their gender. Also called correct pronouns.

Presentation, Presenting: *See* gender presentation.

Primary Sex Characteristics: Anatomical organs that play a direct role in reproduction, such as the genitals.

Pronouns: Small words such as he, she, her, them, and us, which are used to refer to people. In English, there are four common third-person pronoun groups: he/his/him, she/hers/her, they/their/them, and it/its/it. Individual people may decide which of these pronouns they wish to be referred to as, or they may use pronouns that have been more recently coined.

Puberty Blocker: *See* hormone blockers.

Queer: An umbrella term for all people who are not heterosexual, heteroromantic, and cisgender and who self-identify as queer. A sensitive issue because of its history as a slur. Some trans and/or nonbinary people identify as queer, and others do not.

Queering Gender: The act of playing with, deconstructing, transforming, or reclaiming gender, moving it from a heteronormative, patriarchal, and cissexist perspective into a queer perspective.

Radscum: Feminists who exclude, invalidate, or attack trans people, especially toward trans women.

Rape Culture: The social expectations that make rape and sexual assault more socially acceptable or that cause people to deny importance or recognition to acts of sexual assault.

Read: In trans discussions, to correctly perceive someone as their true gender, which may or may not be their assigned sex at birth.

Real-Life Test: A requirement some gatekeepers require trans people to go through before they are willing to provide hormone therapy or surgery; may last anywhere from a few month to several years. This restriction can be dangerous or impossible for some trans people.

Secondary Sex Characteristics: Anatomical features that develop during puberty and that are related to sex hormones but not directly involved in reproduction. Examples include facial hair and rounded breasts.

Sex Change: An outdated and inaccurate term for what is now called transitioning.

Sex Reassignment Surgery: An older term for what is often now called gender confirmation surgery or gender affirmation surgery.

Sexual Orientation: The group of people or genders to which a person can become sexually attracted, if at all.

Singular They: Yes, this is grammatical. "They" is a convenient way to refer to a person of uncertain gender or whose preferred pronouns are unknown. Some people also adopt "they" as their correct pronoun.

Situational Genderfluid: Someone who is situationally genderfluid moves between genders based on their environment. As a subsection of genderfluid, it implies a pattern. (From genderqueeries.)

Skoliosexual: Sexually attracted to gender-variant or nonbinary people. Not to be confused with fetishization of trans or nonbinary people. Some trans and/or nonbinary folks don't like this because of problematic etymology or fetishistic usage, so I don't advise using this.

Social Dysphoria: In trans discussions, dysphoria that is caused by being perceived or treated by other people as an incorrect gender.

Spivak Pronouns: E(y)/eir/em/emself. A set of gender-neutral pronouns.

SRS: Sex reassignment surgery.

Stand-to-Pee: A device used to enable someone to urinate while standing up, in the manner that people with penises sometimes do.

Standards of Care: Full name: "Standards of Care for the Health of Transsexual, Transgender, and Gender Nonconforming People." These are nonbinding guidelines that influence the decisions of many doctors and other gatekeepers in determining whether trans people are allowed to get transitional medical care. Often criticized for being overly strict, for preventing trans youth from transitioning, and for compelling nonbinary trans people to hide or lie about their experiences in order to receive treatment.

Stealth: Living publicly as one's correct gender without being open about the fact that one is trans.

STP: Stand-to-pee.

T: Testosterone

TCR: Thyroid cartilage reduction surgery.

TERF: Trans exclusionary radical feminist. That is, they exclude trans people from their feminist movement and are transphobic and transmisogynistic. *See also* TWERF.

Testosterone: The main androgen hormone in the human body. Supplemental testosterone is sometimes taken by trans people, usually with the intent of achieving a more masculine appearance.

The Surgery: A mysterious and frightening transformation spoken of by cis people who don't know anything about how trans people actually transition.

They (Singular): *See* singular they.

Third Gender: A phrase used in anthropology for genders and gender roles that do not fit the Western constructs of "man" or "woman." The phrase is problematic because of its colonialist or Eurocentric associations.

Tomboy: 1. A woman, usually a young girl, who behaves or dresses in a traditionally masculine or boyish way. 2. Occasionally used as a nonbinary gender or presentation.

Top Surgery: A colloquial term for surgery that corrects one's chest area to better match one's gender presentation.

Trans: Short for transgender or (less often) transsexual.

Trans*: Variant of "trans" that specifically denotes inclusion of nonbinary, genderqueer, and gender-variant people. The asterisk is controversial.

Trans Exclusionary Radical Feminism: A sector of the feminist movement that does not accept trans people, especially trans women.

Trans Man: A man who is also trans.

Trans Woman: A woman who is also trans.

Transexual: Alternative spelling for transsexual.

Transfeminine: Having a gender that is female or feminine-of-center and being trans.

Transgender: An umbrella term for all people and genders that do not match the gender that they were assigned at birth, or that was imposed on them by society, or that they were raised as.

Transition: To change one's presentation to reflect a gender other than the one assigned at birth. Transitioning may include, but does not require, any of the following: changing one's pronouns, wearing different clothing than before, altering one's legal gender, taking hormone therapy, and undergoing surgery.

Transman: Alternative spelling for trans man. Not recommended because it is sometimes seen as implying that "transman" is separate from "man," a form of cissexism.

Transmasculine: Having a gender that is male or masculine-of-center and being trans.

Transmisogyny: Transphobia and misogyny combined, forming an especially virulent form of oppression against trans women and other transfeminine people.

Transphobe: A person who acts, thinks, or speaks with transphobia.

Transphobia: Prejudice, stigma, or discrimination against trans, nonbinary, and/or genderqueer people. Can occur as both an individual attitude and as a widespread social force.

Transsexual: 1. A person whose gender does not match their assigned sex (similar to transgender). 2. A person who has changed, or wishes to change, their anatomy to better reflect their true gender. This is a loaded term and should not be used to refer to someone without their permission. Some transsexual people do not identify as transgender.

Transtrender: A derogatory word used by some trans people to invalidate other trans people's identities. Not recommended for use, as it is frequently associated with respectability politics.

Transvestic Fetishism: A kink in which one derives pleasure (usually sexual) from wearing clothes of a different gender. This phrase is discredited in trans communities because it has often been used to delegitimize trans identities, especially those of trans women.

Transvestite: Old-fashioned word for a person who wears clothing of another gender. Not to be confused with transgender or transsexual. A loaded term, not recommended.

Transwoman: Alternative spelling for trans woman. Not recommended because it is sometimes seen as implying that "transwoman" is separate from "woman," a form of cissexism.

Trigender: 1. Not identifying as male, female, or androgynous but constructing one's own, distinct gender. 2. Having a gender identity that includes or shifts between three or more distinct genders, similarly to bigender.

Truscum: Trans people who invalidate or perpetuate prejudice against other trans people, often by claiming that others are not "truly" trans or "trans enough." This is often related to respectability politics.

Tucking: Moving the genitals into place to make the presence of a penis less obvious.

TWERF: Trans woman exclusionary radical feminist. That is, they exclude trans woman from their feminist movement and are transmisogynistic.

Woman-Born-Woman: A cisgender woman. This term is sometimes used by transphobic people to invalidate trans people, and as such, it is not recommended.

Recommended Resources

Books

She's Not There: A Life in Two Genders, Jenny Finney Boylan

True Selves: Understanding Transsexualism—For Families, Friends, Coworkers, and Helping Professionals, Mildred L. Brown and Chloe Ann Rounsley

Transgender Lives: Complex Stories, Complex Voices, Kirstin Cronn-Mills (Note: a great book for young adults)

Trans Bodies, Trans Selves: A Resource for the Transgender Community, Laura Erickson-Schroth

No! Maybe? Yes! Living My Truth, Grace Anne Stevens

Trangender 101: A Simple Guide to a Complex Issue, Nicholas M. Teich

Visual Media

Lady Valor: The Kristin Beck Story (documentary, 2014)

TransGeneration (TV miniseries, 2005)

Transparent (TV series, 2014)

Organizations

Tiffany Club of New England (check with your local support groups for organizations near you); www.tcne.org

World Professional Association for Transgender Health (WPATH); www.wpath.org

GLAD; GLBTQ legal advocates & defenders; www.glad.org

GLAAD; for over thirty years, GLAAD has been at the forefront of cultural change, accelerating acceptance for the LGBTQ community; www.glaad.org

GLAAD Resources; resources for transgender people in crisis, including organizations and programs; www.glaad.org/ transgender/resources

Parents, Families, and Friends of Lesbians and Gays (PFLAG); www.pflag.org

National Center for Transgender Equality; www.transequality.org

About the Author

Linda DeFruscio-Robinson is the founder of A & A Laser, Electrolysis & Skin Care Associates Inc. of Newtonville, Massachusetts. She has over forty years of electrolysis and skin-care experience and has been practicing laser hair removal for over twenty years. She also has degrees and certifications in dental assisting, hair cutting/styling, facial treatments, etc.—all things that make people feel better about themselves.

A lifelong author, Linda's articles on skin care and hair removal have been published in many national and international journals. Her first full-length book, a memoir called *Cornered: Dr. Richard J. Sharpe as I Knew Him*, was published in 2015. Her children's book, *Ginger and Moe and the Incredible Coincidence*, was published in 2016.

Linda and her husband, Greg, live outside of Boston. The couple has three sons and five grandchildren. They enjoy many activities together in their leisure time, including yoga, day trips, tennis, bowling, and long walks near the ocean.

Kristin Beck
Courtesy of Kristin Beck media@ladyvalor.com

Kristin Beck
Courtesy of Kristin Beck media@ladyvalor.com

Kristin Beck
Courtesy of Kristin Beck media@ladyvalor.com

Kristin Beck and Linda

Merissa Lynn

Linda and Grace Stevens

Linda and Marci Bowers, MD

Rikki Bates
by Bill O'Neill

Persia

Callista

Joanna

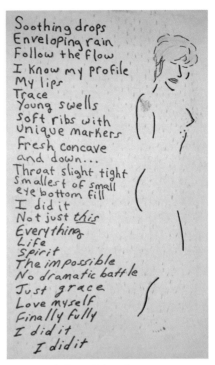

Soothing drops
Enveloping rain
Follow the flow
I know my profile
My lips
Trace
Young swells
Soft ribs with
Unique markers
Fresh concave
and down...
Throat slight tight
Smallest of small
eye bottom fill
I did it
Not just *this*
Everything
Life
Spirit
The impossible
No dramatic battle
Just grace
Love myself
Finally fully
I did it
I did it

Artwork by Joanna

Joanna

Artwork created by Red,
Joanna's grandfather

Sam

Sam

Michelle

Michelle

Erica

Erica

Erica

Erica

Alasandra

Alasandra

Cynthia

Chrissy

Jamie

Debora

Nicki and Lida

Lauren

Holly and Linda

Holly

Ashlee

Ashlee

"Beard from Hell," cartoon by Gina Kamentsky, 1997